MASTERING ADOBE PHOTOSHOP 2025

From Beginner to Expert with Updated Shortcuts, Techniques, and Troubleshooting Tips

Lucas W. Brooks

Acknowledgments

First and foremost, I would like to express my deepest gratitude to my family and friends for their unwavering support and encouragement throughout the process of writing this book. Your belief in me kept me motivated during the long hours of writing, editing, and refining.

A special thanks to the incredible team at Adobe for continuously pushing the boundaries of creativity and for providing such an outstanding software that has inspired millions around the world. Your dedication to innovation has made this book possible.

I would also like to thank my readers—whether you are just beginning your journey with Photoshop or are an experienced user looking to sharpen your skills. Your enthusiasm for learning motivates me to keep creating content that is both practical and inspiring.

To the fellow Photoshop enthusiasts, educators, and designers who have shared their knowledge and insights over the years, I'm deeply grateful. Your contributions to the creative community have shaped the way we all use Photoshop.

A heartfelt thank you to the editorial team, my publisher, and everyone involved in bringing this book to life. Your expertise, professionalism, and attention to detail have been invaluable. This project wouldn't have been possible without your hard work.

Finally, I want to dedicate this book to all the aspiring artists and designers who dare to explore their creativity. May this guide help you unlock your full potential and inspire you to create the amazing work you envision.

Thank you all for being part of this journey.

Table of Contents

Introduction

The journey of creativity begins with the tools you choose to bring your ideas to life. For digital artists, designers, photographers, and creative professionals, Adobe Photoshop has long been the gold standard in image editing and graphic design. With each new version, Photoshop continues to push the boundaries of what's possible, and Adobe Photoshop 2025 is no exception. Whether you're opening the software for the first time or are already a seasoned user, there's always something new to discover.

Adobe Photoshop 2025 is a powerful suite of features that can transform an idea into something extraordinary. It's not just a program for retouching photos; it's a canvas for digital painters, a layout tool for designers, and a hub for visual storytelling. The beauty of Photoshop lies in its versatility—it can accommodate everything from quick fixes to complex, multi-layered projects, and it can be applied across industries, from marketing and advertising to animation and web design.

In this book, we're going to explore the depth of Photoshop 2025 and help you unlock its full potential. Whether you're a beginner unsure of where to start or an advanced user looking to refine your skills, this guide will walk you through each feature in a way that's easy to understand and immediately applicable to your work. Photoshop can feel overwhelming, especially when faced with a vast array of tools and functions, but this guide will break things down in a way that is clear and digestible. Think of this as your personal roadmap to mastering the software.

What makes Photoshop 2025 even more exciting is the introduction of new features and improvements that make your creative process smoother and more efficient. Whether it's the enhanced AI-powered tools, the updated user interface, or the new shortcuts designed to speed up your workflow, this version is all about making your experience more intuitive. Adobe has listened to feedback from users, and the result is a product that makes it easier than ever to create stunning visuals. The user interface is designed to streamline your workflow, meaning you spend less time searching for tools and more time focused on your craft.

Throughout this book, we will not only cover the basics of how to use Photoshop but also dive into advanced techniques that can take your designs to the next level. You'll learn how to use the tools in ways that maximize their capabilities, bringing your creative vision to life with precision and skill. From manipulating images to creating complex designs, we'll explore how each function plays a role in your artistic journey. You'll discover how the settings, tools, and layers all work together seamlessly to produce results you never thought possible.

This guide is built for creators like you, those who want to master the craft of digital design and photography. With updated shortcuts, tips, and troubleshooting advice, it's designed to help you navigate Photoshop 2025 and overcome any challenges you might encounter. No matter where you are in your creative journey, this book will provide the knowledge and inspiration to push you forward.

Now, let's dive into this exciting world of creative possibilities and make Photoshop 2025 your ultimate tool for visual expression. Get ready to learn, experiment, and discover all the incredible things you can do with this powerful software.

Overview of Adobe Photoshop 2025

Adobe Photoshop 2025 marks another significant leap forward in the evolution of digital art, photography, and design. For over three decades, Photoshop has been the undisputed leader in image manipulation and graphic design software, empowering creators across the globe to turn their ideas into professional-grade visuals. With each new version, Adobe has fine-tuned the platform to meet the needs of its ever-growing community of artists, designers, photographers, and even casual users. Photoshop 2025 is no different. It's a software suite that continues to blend cutting-edge technology with user-centric design, offering an experience that is both intuitive and powerful.

One of the most notable advancements in Photoshop 2025 is its enhanced integration with artificial intelligence (AI). Adobe has incorporated AI-driven features that improve accuracy, speed, and ease of use. These AI tools help automate repetitive tasks, making it possible for users to focus more on their creativity and less on the technical side of things. For example, the AI-powered selection tools in Photoshop 2025 are more precise than ever, making it easier to select objects, isolate subjects, or remove unwanted elements from an image. This is a game-changer for professionals who need to work with complex compositions and need to save time without sacrificing quality.

Photoshop 2025 also brings a more streamlined and customizable user interface. The layout has been optimized for both new and experienced users, with options to tailor the workspace to suit individual needs. The toolbars and menus are more intuitive, meaning you can spend less time looking for the right tool and more time working on your project. The design improvements have made the workspace even more flexible, allowing users to focus on their creative tasks rather than navigating a cluttered interface.

In addition to UI improvements, Photoshop 2025 introduces new tools that push the boundaries of creative possibilities. The new, upgraded neural filters give users access to a range of innovative effects and enhancements. For example, you can now easily change the facial expressions of people in photos, adjust the age or gaze direction, or apply realistic makeup effects—all with a few clicks. This feature is especially useful for portrait photographers and digital artists who want to make quick adjustments without the need for detailed manual editing.

Another exciting addition is the new 3D tools, which allow for more advanced modeling, texturing, and rendering. These tools are perfect for designers working on product mockups, animation, and motion graphics. With these features, Adobe has closed the gap between Photoshop and other specialized 3D software, making Photoshop a more versatile tool for all types of visual creators. The ability to combine 3D models with 2D images allows users to create more realistic and dynamic compositions.

The collaboration features introduced in Photoshop 2025 are another standout. These tools make it easier for teams to collaborate on projects, share files, and work in real-time, no matter where they are. With the increasing demand for remote work and online collaboration, this new feature ensures that creatives can work together seamlessly. Photoshop now supports cloud-based saving and syncing, allowing users to access their work from any device, at any time, and make real-time adjustments during collaborative sessions.

Adobe has also made strides in performance optimization in Photoshop 2025. The software now runs faster and more efficiently, even on older machines. The enhanced GPU acceleration ensures smooth performance when working with complex files, while memory management improvements make it possible to work with larger images without running into slowdowns or crashes. Whether you're working with high-resolution images, complex 3D models, or multiple layers, Photoshop 2025 is designed to handle the most demanding tasks with ease.

Furthermore, Photoshop 2025 introduces enhanced video editing tools, allowing users to make advanced edits to video clips within the same interface they use for photos. This is particularly useful for content creators who need to combine photo and video content into their projects. It's an all-in-one solution that saves time and allows for more seamless workflows.

Overall, Adobe Photoshop 2025 offers an unprecedented level of control, creativity, and efficiency, all wrapped in a beautifully designed and user-friendly package. It's an essential tool for anyone who wants to create stunning visuals, whether they are working on a personal project, commercial design, or professional photography.

Why Photoshop is Essential for Creators

There's a reason Adobe Photoshop is considered the go-to software for creators across the world. It's not just a tool—it's an ecosystem that supports all types of creative professionals. Whether you're a photographer looking to enhance an image, a designer working on a logo, an illustrator crafting digital art, or even an animator building a scene, Photoshop provides everything you need to bring your vision to life.

The versatility of Photoshop makes it a vital tool for creators of all kinds. From fine-tuning details in photographs to designing intricate layouts and even creating digital artwork from scratch, Photoshop is designed to handle any task a creator might throw at it. There's no other software that offers the same combination of power, flexibility, and tools that Photoshop does, making it indispensable for professionals in creative fields.

For photographers, Photoshop is the ultimate tool for image manipulation. The software allows you to adjust exposure, contrast, color, and sharpness with precision, and its non-destructive editing capabilities allow for maximum flexibility. You can fix issues like underexposed or overexposed images, remove distractions, and enhance details—all without permanently altering the original image. The software also offers a wide variety of retouching tools that allow you to remove blemishes, smooth skin, and even change the lighting in a photograph. It's a powerful tool for anyone who wants to take their photography to the next level.

Graphic designers rely heavily on Photoshop because of its robust vector and raster capabilities. Designers can create everything from detailed illustrations to typography and logos. With Photoshop, you have the ability to create and manipulate vector shapes, apply custom gradients, and work with typography in a way that's not possible in other image editing software. The layering system allows for complex compositions and makes it easy to adjust individual elements without affecting the entire design. Additionally, with Photoshop's ability to handle both 2D and 3D objects, designers can bring their ideas to life in ways that were once reserved for specialized programs.

Illustrators, too, find Photoshop indispensable. The software offers a wide array of brushes and painting tools, allowing artists to mimic traditional painting techniques while enjoying the benefits of digital tools. Whether you're sketching, shading, or painting, Photoshop gives you the freedom to create with endless possibilities. Its brushes can be customized to suit any artist's style, making it a powerful tool for everything from fine art to digital comics.

Motion graphics artists and animators also turn to Photoshop because of its ability to work with animated assets. Photoshop now includes tools that allow for the creation and editing of animated gifs, as well as importing and editing video files. This makes it a one-stop-shop for anyone working in motion graphics, as they can combine still imagery with animation and video seamlessly.

The rise of social media and digital content creation has further cemented Photoshop's importance. Influencers, content creators, and marketers rely on Photoshop to create eye-catching graphics, edit photos, and design visual assets for websites, ads, and posts. With its extensive set of web and UI design tools, Photoshop is often used in combination with other software to create full-scale designs, from websites to mobile apps.

Photoshop's cloud integration and collaboration features have made it easier for creators to work together, even when they are not in the same location. The ability to work on projects across devices and share files instantly has transformed the way many creative teams operate. This added flexibility makes Photoshop essential for freelancers and design teams who need to share files, gather feedback, and collaborate remotely.

Ultimately, Photoshop isn't just a tool; it's a platform for creative professionals. It empowers creators to bring their ideas to life, offering them a flexible, powerful, and efficient way to work. The depth of features, the incredible support network, and the continuous updates ensure that Photoshop remains not only relevant but essential for anyone looking to produce professional-quality designs, photos, illustrations, and videos. For creators who want to make their mark in the digital world, Photoshop 2025 is a must-have in their creative toolkit.

What's New in Photoshop 2025

Adobe Photoshop 2025 brings a fresh wave of innovations designed to simplify workflows, enhance creativity, and boost productivity. The new version of this already powerful software continues Adobe's tradition of evolving with the demands of its users, introducing a variety of exciting features that not only cater to the seasoned professional but also empower beginners to tackle complex projects with ease. In this latest release, Photoshop introduces a host of features focused on automation, AI-assisted tools, improved collaboration, and an even more streamlined interface, all aimed at making the creative process faster and more intuitive.

One of the most groundbreaking updates in Photoshop 2025 is the improved AI integration, making tasks that once required painstaking manual effort now quicker and more accurate. For instance, the new AI-powered selection tools have significantly enhanced the software's ability to automatically detect and isolate objects in images. Whether you are working with intricate subjects like hair or complex backgrounds, Photoshop's AI tools make it easier than ever to make precise selections. The AI-based object removal feature allows for seamless and realistic deletions of unwanted elements within an image, with the software intelligently filling in the gaps. This makes tedious tasks such as background removal or subject isolation not only simpler but also faster.

Another major improvement is the revamped neural filters. These filters now offer even more creative control, including options to adjust facial expressions in portrait photography, enhance the lighting of an image in real-time, and even change the seasons or time of day in an image without having to manually edit it. These features are an incredible resource for photographers and digital artists, allowing for easy and dramatic transformations of images with just a few clicks.

In Photoshop 2025, the 3D tools have been enhanced to include even more advanced capabilities for creating 3D objects, as well as integrating 3D textures into 2D designs. This is a game-changer for product designers, animators, and graphic designers who often need to create 3D mockups or visualizations.

Photoshop now offers a much more fluid and accessible environment for blending 3D elements with traditional 2D artwork, giving creators the flexibility to experiment with depth, texture, and light in a way that was once the domain of specialized software.

Another major highlight in this version is the overhaul of collaboration features. Given the increasing shift towards remote work, Adobe has made significant strides in making it easier for teams to collaborate directly within Photoshop. With cloud-based synchronization, you can now share files with colleagues or clients and work on them in real-time. Photoshop 2025 also supports improved commenting and feedback tools, allowing multiple users to add comments directly to the file, making the review process smoother and more efficient.

In terms of performance, Photoshop 2025 is faster than ever before. GPU acceleration is even more finely tuned, ensuring that even the most complex projects—such as high-resolution images or multi-layered compositions—are handled smoothly. The updated memory management system ensures that users can work with large files without worrying about slowdowns, even on older machines. Adobe has also optimized the software for the latest hardware, meaning those with newer systems will see even faster processing and rendering speeds.

Additionally, the video editing capabilities in Photoshop have been significantly expanded. Now, users can edit video frames, add graphics or text, and even create animations within the same interface they use for photo editing. This is a fantastic feature for content creators who work with multimedia, allowing them to seamlessly combine still images and videos for dynamic, engaging content creation.

With Photoshop 2025, Adobe has once again proven that it is committed to staying ahead of the curve, offering a suite of tools that cater to both newcomers and advanced users. These new features, combined with the existing robust tools that Photoshop is known for, make this version an essential upgrade for anyone serious about digital creation. Whether you're refining your photos, crafting intricate designs, or experimenting with new techniques, Photoshop 2025 is designed to help you achieve professional-quality results with speed and ease.

How to Use This Book

This book is designed with one goal in mind: to guide you through the ins and outs of Adobe Photoshop 2025, from basic to advanced techniques, all while helping you navigate the new features that make this version so powerful. Whether you're completely new to Photoshop or already an experienced user looking to expand your knowledge, this guide provides a structured and comprehensive approach to mastering the software.

The book is divided into well-organized chapters, each focusing on a specific aspect of Photoshop. You'll begin by getting comfortable with the user interface and learning the essential tools, and gradually progress to more advanced topics like working with layers, 3D objects, and AI-powered features. The structure is designed to build upon itself—starting with the basics and moving toward more complex workflows, ensuring you get a deep understanding of the program step by step.

Each chapter is filled with practical exercises and real-world examples, designed to help you apply what you've learned immediately. Whether you're following along with a tutorial or working on your own project, these exercises will reinforce your skills and give you the hands-on experience needed to feel confident in using Photoshop. The examples cover a wide range of creative disciplines, so no matter your focus—whether it's photography, design, or digital art—you'll find content that's directly applicable to your field.

As you work through the chapters, you'll also find tips and tricks throughout the book. These are designed to help you save time, improve your workflow, and make the most of Photoshop's many tools. Photoshop is a vast program, and there are always shortcuts or lesser-known features that can significantly improve your efficiency. This book will not only teach you how to use the tools, but also how to use them in the most effective and efficient way.

You'll also find a section dedicated to troubleshooting common problems and performance issues. Photoshop is a powerful program, and at times it may run into technical difficulties, especially when working with large files or complex projects. This book will help you understand how to solve issues related to crashes, slow performance, or errors, ensuring that you can keep working without unnecessary disruptions.

Each chapter will also touch on the new features introduced in Photoshop 2025. As Adobe continues to innovate, it's essential to stay up-to-date with the latest advancements in the software. This book will ensure you're able to integrate the new AI-driven tools, advanced 3D features, and enhanced collaboration options into your workflow seamlessly.

For those new to Photoshop, the book starts with the basics—getting you familiar with the interface, understanding the layout, and walking you through fundamental tools. As you progress, you'll learn more advanced techniques, such as working with multiple layers, using blending modes, and even creating custom brushes. For more experienced users, you can skip ahead to chapters on advanced techniques or dive deeper into the new features introduced in Photoshop 2025.

By the end of this book, you will not only have mastered the basics of Photoshop 2025, but also developed the skills to take on more complex and creative projects with confidence. Whether you're looking to refine your photography skills, enhance your design capabilities, or create stunning digital artwork, this book is your roadmap to becoming a Photoshop pro. Each chapter is carefully designed to ensure that by the time you finish, you'll be ready to unlock the full potential of this incredible software.

Chapter 1: Getting Started with Photoshop 2025

Starting your journey with Photoshop 2025 opens up an exciting world of creative possibilities. Whether you're just getting started or you've used previous versions of Photoshop, diving into this updated version is sure to spark your imagination and enhance your design skills. The interface is designed to be intuitive, yet powerful enough to handle complex tasks, so getting the hang of it doesn't take long. This chapter will guide you through everything you need to know to get up and running with Photoshop 2025, from setting up the software to creating your first project.

As with any powerful tool, understanding how to navigate Photoshop's workspace is essential. Adobe has streamlined the interface to make it more user-friendly, ensuring that you can focus on your creative work instead of getting lost in complicated menus. Upon opening Photoshop 2025, the first thing you'll notice is the clean, organized workspace, where key elements like the menu bar, tool panel, and workspace are easily accessible. The default workspace is well-suited for most users, but Photoshop also allows you to customize your workspace layout to fit your specific needs. Whether you're working on a photo edit, graphic design, or illustration, Photoshop ensures that everything you need is within reach.

Creating a new document in Photoshop 2025 is straightforward. The "New Document" dialog box lets you customize your project settings, including the document size, resolution, color mode, and more. If you're working on a print project, you'll want to set the resolution to 300 DPI to ensure high-quality output. For digital projects, 72 DPI is sufficient. You'll also have the option to choose between various presets, such as A4, letter-sized, or custom dimensions, depending on the type of project you're working on. Understanding these settings ensures that your project looks its best, whether it's for print or web use.

Once your document is set up, you'll dive into the core of Photoshop—its tools. The tool panel on the left side of the screen holds a variety of tools that are essential for editing and creating. Each tool is designed to accomplish a specific task, from basic selections and brushwork to more complex manipulations like content-aware fill and image retouching. While it might seem overwhelming at first, learning how to use these tools will unlock your full creative potential. You can start with the selection tools, which are ideal for isolating parts of an image that you want to edit. Whether you need to adjust color, apply filters, or remove unwanted objects, mastering the selection tools is crucial for any Photoshop project.

Photoshop 2025 also comes with a few new features that enhance the user experience. For example, the updated interface makes it easier to access commonly used features like layers, adjustment tools, and blending modes. If you're familiar with previous versions of Photoshop, the transitions will feel familiar, but the enhancements in 2025 ensure a smoother, faster experience. Additionally, with the new cloud-based syncing feature, you can save your work directly to the cloud and access it from any device. This is especially useful if you work across multiple devices or need to collaborate with others on a project.

Getting started with Photoshop 2025 is just the beginning of a rewarding creative journey. As you familiarize yourself with the workspace, tools, and features, you'll be ready to take on more advanced projects and techniques. From simple photo adjustments to complex digital artwork, Photoshop offers an incredible range of possibilities. The next steps are yours to explore, and with the foundation laid in this chapter, you'll be able to jump straight into your projects with confidence. It's time to let your creativity flow and begin making your mark with Photoshop 2025!

Introduction to the Photoshop Workspace

The workspace is the heart of Adobe Photoshop, where all your creative work happens. When you first open Photoshop 2025, you'll be greeted with a fresh, clean interface designed to maximize productivity while keeping the creative process at the forefront. Understanding how to navigate and personalize the workspace is key to working efficiently and comfortably. The layout of Photoshop's workspace is flexible and fully customizable, allowing you to adjust it to suit your personal workflow and preferences. Whether you're editing a photo, designing graphics, or creating digital art, mastering the workspace will significantly enhance your experience with the software.

When you first launch Photoshop 2025, the default workspace is set to "Essentials," which is perfect for most users, but knowing how to customize the layout for different types of projects is incredibly useful. The workspace consists of several main components: the Menu Bar, Options Bar, Tool Panel, Document Window, and Panels. Each of these parts plays a crucial role in your workflow, and knowing how they function will allow you to quickly find and use the tools you need.

The Menu Bar at the top of the screen contains all the main commands, such as file operations, editing functions, and image adjustments. It's your go-to area for performing global tasks like opening or saving files, applying filters, or accessing Photoshop's settings. The Options Bar, located just below the Menu Bar, dynamically changes depending on the tool you select, providing relevant options and settings. For example, when you choose the Brush tool, the Options Bar will display different brush settings, allowing you to customize the tool without needing to open other menus.

The Tool Panel on the left side of the screen is where most of your editing tools live. It contains tools for selecting, painting, retouching, and manipulating your images. You can expand and collapse groups of tools to keep the panel clean, making it easier to focus on the tools you use most. If you're unsure where a tool is located, you can press the Shift key and cycle through tool groups to discover more options.

One of Photoshop 2025's most notable upgrades is its customizable workspace. If you're accustomed to working in a specific way, Photoshop allows you to tailor your layout to fit your needs. The first step to customizing your workspace is by accessing the Window menu, where you can choose which panels you want to display. Panels are sections of the interface that help you manage and organize your work. You'll find panels for Layers, History, Properties, Actions, and much more. You can dock these panels on the sides of the workspace, or float them freely on the screen, depending on your preference.

Another important feature of the workspace is the ability to save your workspace layout. After arranging the panels, toolbars, and options the way you want, you can save this configuration as your own custom workspace. This means that every time you open Photoshop, it will load your preferred layout, ensuring consistency and efficiency in your workflow.

Photoshop 2025 has made it even easier to switch between different workspaces. If you are working on a specific task like painting, photography, or 3D design, you can switch to a preset workspace tailored to that activity. You can access these workspaces through the Window > Workspace menu. By switching between workspaces, you can quickly access the panels and tools needed for that particular task, without having to manually rearrange the layout.

Another important aspect of the workspace is the Document Window. This is where you'll see and interact with your image. When you open a file, it appears here, and you can zoom in and out, pan across your project, and make edits. The Document Window is where the action happens, and understanding how to manage it will make working in Photoshop more efficient. For example, you can use the Tab key to hide or show all panels, giving you a larger workspace to focus on the image itself.

To further enhance your workflow, Photoshop 2025 also allows you to split the workspace by opening multiple documents at once. You can view them side by side or in different tabs, making it easy to reference multiple files during a project. This is especially useful for projects that require you to compare images or work on a composite.

Mastering the Photoshop workspace is the first step toward working more efficiently. Once you feel comfortable navigating the layout and customizing it to your needs, you'll find that the software becomes a much more intuitive tool for your creative projects.

Understanding Photoshop Preferences & Settings

One of the most powerful aspects of Photoshop 2025 is its ability to be tailored to suit your specific needs and workflow. The Preferences menu in Photoshop holds a vast array of settings that allow you to customize nearly every aspect of the software, from performance to interface behavior. Setting up Photoshop correctly from the start will ensure that you can work with the highest level of efficiency and ease.

When you first install Photoshop 2025, the software comes with a set of default settings that work well for most users. However, you may want to adjust certain preferences to align the software with your personal workflow and the types of projects you typically work on. To access the Preferences menu, click on Edit in the Menu Bar and select Preferences, or press Ctrl + K (Windows) or Cmd + K (Mac) as a shortcut.

One of the first areas you might want to adjust is the Performance section. Photoshop is a resource-intensive application, especially when working with large files or complex projects. By going into the Performance settings, you can allocate more RAM to Photoshop, enabling it to run more smoothly. If you're working with high-resolution images or intricate designs, this adjustment can make a significant difference in how the software performs. You can also adjust GPU settings, which help Photoshop run faster when handling graphics-heavy tasks like 3D rendering or applying filters.

Next, you'll want to check out the File Handling preferences. Photoshop 2025 offers several options for managing how files are opened and saved. You can set it to automatically save recovery files, so you don't lose work in case of a crash. You can also control the default file format for saving, ensuring you're always saving in the most appropriate format for your needs, whether it's PSD, TIFF, PNG, or another file type.

Another critical section of the Preferences menu is the Units & Rulers tab. If you're working on design projects for print, setting your ruler units to inches or millimeters can be helpful. On the other hand, if you're creating web graphics, you might prefer to set the units to pixels. Adjusting this setting ensures that measurements and guides are accurate for the specific medium you're designing for.

For designers and photographers, the Transparency & Gamut preferences are also important. You can customize the default settings for transparent areas in your projects, such as how Photoshop displays the grid for transparent backgrounds. Understanding these settings ensures that your images appear as expected when you view them on different devices or print them out.

Photoshop's Interface preferences allow you to fine-tune the look and feel of the program itself. You can change the color theme of the workspace, switch between light and dark modes, and adjust the UI size for different screen resolutions. If you work long hours on your projects, choosing a theme that feels comfortable to your eyes can make a significant difference in your productivity and comfort.

Finally, there's the Shortcuts section, where you can customize keyboard shortcuts to speed up your workflow. Photoshop comes with a comprehensive set of default shortcuts, but if there are certain functions you use frequently, you can create custom shortcuts that make accessing these tools even faster.

Setting up Photoshop 2025 by adjusting these preferences will ensure that the software behaves exactly the way you want it to, improving your efficiency and productivity. By customizing the settings to your needs, you can reduce friction and create a more personalized workspace that helps you focus on what you do best—being creative. Whether you're a photographer, designer, or illustrator, taking the time to adjust your preferences will provide you with a smoother, more enjoyable experience with Photoshop 2025.

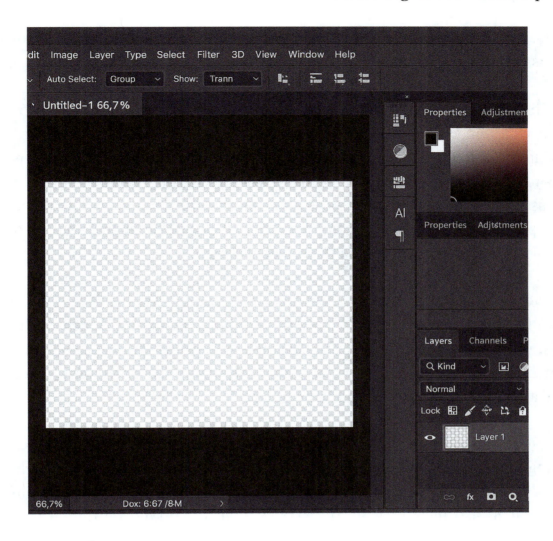

How to Create a New Document

Creating a new document in Photoshop 2025 is the first step to beginning any project, whether you're working on a photo edit, graphic design, or digital painting. Photoshop's "New Document" dialog box offers a variety of customizable options that let you set the parameters for your project right from the start. Understanding these settings and choosing the right ones is essential for ensuring your project meets the required specifications, whether it's for print, web, or any other medium.

When you launch Photoshop and select File > New, the "New Document" dialog box will appear. Here, you will be prompted to define several key settings before you start your project. Each of these settings plays a crucial role in determining the quality, appearance, and file size of your work. Let's go through each of these options to help you understand how to tailor your document settings to your needs.

The first thing you'll notice is the Preset dropdown menu. Photoshop 2025 comes with a wide range of preset document sizes, including options for standard paper sizes (like A4, letter, or legal), web dimensions (like 1920x1080 for HD), and even artboard sizes for various design needs. If you are starting with a common format, such as creating a social media post, you can choose the appropriate preset here. These presets save you time by automatically filling in the dimensions, resolution, and color mode settings based on the selected option.

However, if you need a custom document size, simply set the Width and Height manually. You can specify the size in different units, including inches, millimeters, pixels, or centimeters. The unit of measurement depends on the project's intended output. For print projects, inches or millimeters are most commonly used, while pixels are the standard unit for digital content.

Next, you'll set the Resolution, which is one of the most important choices when creating a new document. Resolution refers to the number of pixels per inch (PPI), and it determines the level of detail in your image. A higher resolution means more detail, but it also increases the file size. If you're working on digital content, a resolution of 72 PPI is usually sufficient, as this is the standard for screen display. However, for print projects, 300 PPI is the standard resolution for high-quality prints. If you set a lower resolution, your image may appear pixelated or blurry when printed, so it's crucial to select the right resolution based on the output medium.

Below the resolution setting is the Color Mode option. This determines the color space your document will use. Photoshop offers several options here, but the two most common are RGB and CMYK. RGB (Red, Green, Blue) is used for projects intended to be viewed on screens, such as websites or digital art, because it is based on light and the color combinations that are possible on monitors. CMYK (Cyan, Magenta, Yellow, Black) is used for print projects, as printers use these four colors to create a full spectrum of colors. Selecting the correct color mode at the start is crucial because it affects how the colors in your document will appear on different devices or when printed.

You'll also notice options for Bit Depth, which refers to the number of colors in the image. Photoshop allows you to choose between 8-bit, 16-bit, or 32-bit depth. The higher the bit depth, the more colors can be displayed, which is useful for projects requiring rich, detailed color transitions (such as in high-end photography). Most users will find 8-bit depth sufficient for their work, but for professional photographers or artists working with complex gradients, 16-bit depth can provide better color representation.

Once you've set these basic options, Photoshop also offers advanced settings such as Background Contents. This lets you choose the background color for your document. You can select White, Background Color, or Transparent. For example, if you're working on a graphic design project where the background needs to remain invisible (such as for use on websites), choosing Transparent will give you a clean, transparent canvas.

At this point, you may also notice an option for creating an Artboard. Artboards are helpful when working with multiple canvases within a single project. They allow you to design multiple items (like web pages or design components) in one Photoshop file, with each artboard functioning as a separate workspace. This is especially useful for UI/UX designers, as it helps them stay organized and manage different design elements within a single document.

Finally, after customizing all the necessary settings for your new document, click Create, and Photoshop will open a fresh, blank canvas with the parameters you've specified. Now, you're ready to begin working on your project.

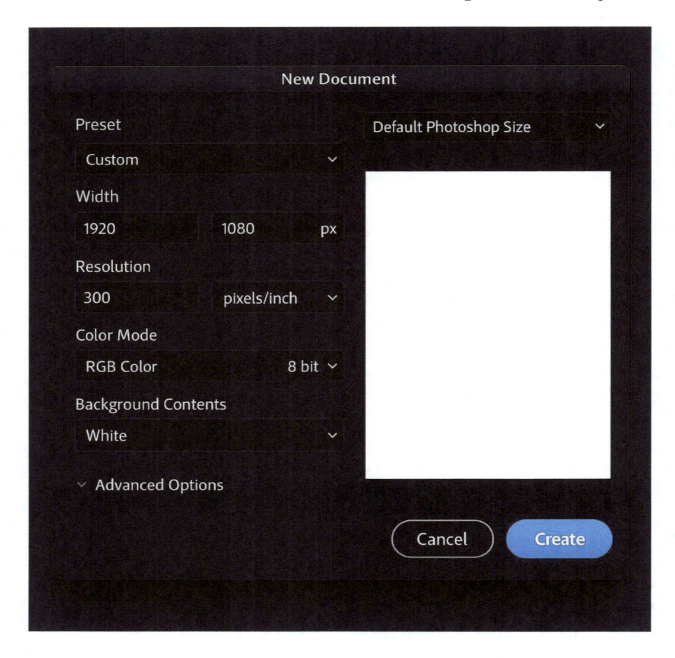

Importing Files and Opening Projects

Once you've created a new document, the next logical step is importing files and opening existing projects. Photoshop is a versatile software that supports a wide variety of file formats, giving you the flexibility to work with different types of content. Whether you're bringing in images to edit, creating a new composition with multiple elements, or opening an existing project to continue working on it, understanding how to import and open files is crucial to getting your work done efficiently.

To import an image into your document, simply go to File > Open, then navigate to the file location on your computer. You can open multiple files simultaneously by holding down Ctrl (Cmd on Mac) while selecting multiple files in the file browser. Photoshop supports various image formats, including JPG, PNG, TIFF, GIF, BMP, and PSD, which is Photoshop's native file format. These formats cover most of the image types you'll encounter in everyday use, from photographs to graphics.

The JPG (JPEG) format is one of the most common image formats used on the web. It's great for photographs and images with a wide range of colors and gradients. However, JPG files use lossy compression, which means some image quality may be lost when saving or resizing the file. This makes JPG an excellent format for web use, where smaller file sizes are needed, but not the best choice for projects that require high image quality, such as print work.

If you need to preserve the highest possible image quality, consider using the TIFF format, especially for print projects. TIFF files are uncompressed or use lossless compression, ensuring that no data is lost when saving the file. This makes TIFF a great option for high-quality images or professional photography that requires fine details. Keep in mind, however, that TIFF files tend to be larger in size than JPGs, which may impact storage or sharing capabilities.

PNG (Portable Network Graphics) is another popular format, particularly for web graphics. Unlike JPG, PNG files use lossless compression, meaning no image quality is lost when saving. PNG also supports transparency, making it a go-to choice for images that need a transparent background, such as logos or icons.

Photoshop's native PSD format is ideal when working on projects within Photoshop itself. This format allows you to save your work with all layers, adjustment settings, masks, and other elements intact, enabling you to make changes and edits later without losing quality. When you save a file in PSD format, you maintain the flexibility to work with all the components of your design, which is essential for complex projects.

If you're working on a vector-based project, you may also need to import files in AI (Adobe Illustrator) or EPS (Encapsulated PostScript) formats. These file types retain the scalability of vector graphics, making them ideal for logos, illustrations, and other design elements that need to be resized without losing quality.

After selecting a file to import, Photoshop will open it in a new tab or window, depending on your workspace settings. You can drag and drop files directly into the workspace, or use File > Place Embedded or Place Linked to insert images or other assets directly into your document. The key difference between these two options is that Place Embedded imports a file directly into your Photoshop document, whereas Place Linked maintains a link to the original file location, meaning any changes made to the original file will automatically update in Photoshop.

Importing files into Photoshop is seamless, but understanding the different file formats and when to use each one can help you streamline your workflow and ensure that your project maintains its quality, size, and compatibility. Whether you're working with high-resolution images, vector graphics, or raw photo files, Photoshop makes it easy to open and manipulate your assets to fit your creative needs.

Chapter 2: Mastering Basic Tools & Techniques

The power of Photoshop lies in the tools you use to bring your ideas to life. As you dive into the world of digital design and image editing, mastering the basic tools is crucial to unlocking the full potential of Photoshop. These tools are the foundation of everything you'll create, whether it's a simple retouch or an intricate piece of art. In this chapter, we'll take a closer look at the essential tools and techniques that will help you navigate your Photoshop projects with ease and confidence.

Photoshop is equipped with a vast array of tools, each designed for specific tasks. The Selection Tools are your first stop. These tools allow you to isolate specific parts of an image so you can edit them without affecting the rest of the project. The Rectangular Marquee Tool and Elliptical Marquee Tool are great for selecting geometric areas, while the Lasso Tool and Polygonal Lasso Tool give you the flexibility to make freehand selections. If you need precision, the Magic Wand Tool quickly selects pixels based on color similarity, and the Quick Selection Tool makes it easy to paint over areas for selection. Once you get the hang of these tools, your ability to isolate and manipulate parts of your images will increase exponentially.

After selecting areas of your image, you'll often want to refine them. The Brush Tool is your go-to for painting and making adjustments. Whether you're adding color, softening edges, or even creating textured effects, the Brush Tool offers a wide range of brushes that can mimic traditional art techniques like watercolor, oil paint, and charcoal. The flexibility to adjust size, hardness, and opacity gives you full control over your strokes, making this tool essential for artists and designers alike. Experimenting with different brushes and settings will open up a world of creative possibilities, whether you're painting a background or retouching a portrait.

Another powerful tool in your Photoshop toolkit is the Clone Stamp Tool, which allows you to duplicate parts of an image and paint them over other areas. This is particularly useful for removing unwanted elements or seamlessly filling in gaps. The Healing Brush Tool works similarly but goes a step further by blending the texture, lighting, and shading of the sampled pixels with the surrounding areas, making it perfect for touching up blemishes or repairing damaged photos.

Working with Layers is another crucial aspect of mastering Photoshop. Layers allow you to work on individual elements of your design without permanently altering the underlying image. With layers, you can stack elements, adjust their order, and apply various effects, all while maintaining flexibility. Photoshop's Layer Styles—such as drop shadows, glows, and bevels—add depth and dimension to your designs, while Adjustment Layers let you modify colors and tones without affecting the original image. Layers are the foundation of non-destructive editing, meaning you can always go back and make changes without losing any of your original work.

As you become more comfortable with these tools, you'll begin to notice how seamlessly they all work together. The Eraser Tool, for instance, can remove parts of an image or layer, and combined with layer masks, it gives you even more control over which parts of your design remain visible. With the Gradient Tool, you can create smooth transitions between colors, which is especially useful for backgrounds or creating shading effects. Each of these tools plays a critical role in the Photoshop workflow, and as you practice, you'll find that they become second nature.

The basic tools in Photoshop 2025 are the building blocks of your creative process. Whether you're editing a photo, designing graphics, or creating digital art, these tools will be your go-to for nearly every project. Mastering them will not only make you more efficient but also expand your creative horizons. The more you use these tools, the more your confidence will grow, and soon, you'll be able to handle even the most complex designs with ease. Let's dive deeper into the power these tools hold and begin experimenting with them to elevate your projects to the next level.

Overview of Selection Tools

Mastering Photoshop's selection tools is one of the most important steps toward becoming proficient with the software. Whether you're isolating a subject from a background, adjusting specific areas of an image, or working with intricate details, understanding how to use selection tools effectively will give you the flexibility and control you need. Photoshop provides a variety of selection tools, each tailored to different tasks. The Rectangular Marquee Tool, Lasso Tool, Magic Wand Tool, and Quick Selection Tool are the primary tools you'll use to select parts of your images, and each one offers unique functionality.

The Rectangular Marquee Tool is one of the simplest yet most essential tools for making basic selections. As the name suggests, it allows you to select rectangular or square areas of an image. To use this tool, simply click and drag to form a rectangular selection. This is great for selecting specific sections of an image, such as when you need to crop or adjust a portion of a photo. If you need a perfect square, hold down the Shift key while making the selection to constrain the shape.

For more freeform selections, the Lasso Tool gives you full control. This tool allows you to trace around any part of an image with your mouse or stylus, creating a custom selection. While holding the mouse button down, you can draw any shape around the area you wish to select. The Polygonal Lasso Tool is a variation that creates straight-line segments, which is helpful when selecting angular shapes or edges. The Magnetic Lasso Tool is another variation that automatically snaps to edges, making it ideal for selecting subjects with clear boundaries against a contrasting background. This is particularly useful when working with objects that have defined edges like portraits or product images.

If you need to select large or complex areas quickly, the Magic Wand Tool is the way to go. This tool selects areas based on color similarity, which is especially useful when working with uniform backgrounds or when you want to select objects with a specific color. By clicking on a color in your image, Photoshop will automatically select areas with similar tones, making it easier to isolate elements. You can adjust the Tolerance setting to control how similar the selected pixels need to be in order to be included in the selection. A low tolerance will select only very similar colors, while a higher tolerance will select a broader range of colors.

For even more control, the Quick Selection Tool works like a paintbrush, allowing you to "paint" over an area to select it. Photoshop will automatically detect the edges of the object as you brush over it, making it perfect for irregular shapes or when you need to refine your selection. This tool is often faster and more efficient than manually tracing with the Lasso Tool, especially when working with more complex images.

Each of these selection tools can be modified with options like Add to Selection or Subtract from Selection, giving you more flexibility in refining your selection. By combining the power of these tools, you can tackle even the most challenging selection tasks with ease. As you become more comfortable with these options, you'll find that your workflow becomes more efficient, allowing you to focus on the creative aspects of your projects.

Paint and Edit Tools

Once you've selected an area of an image, the next step is to make adjustments, paint, or retouch. Photoshop's Brush Tool, Clone Stamp Tool, and Healing Brush Tool are essential for performing these tasks, and each has its own set of capabilities that can enhance your creative workflow.

The Brush Tool is perhaps the most versatile tool in Photoshop. It allows you to paint on your image, and you can use it for a wide variety of purposes—painting backgrounds, adding texture, or even creating detailed artwork. The Brush Tool comes with a range of brush presets, but you can also create and customize your own brushes. You can adjust the size, hardness, opacity, and flow of the brush, giving you complete control over how the paint is applied. For example, you can use a soft, low-opacity brush to add gentle shading, or a hard, high-opacity brush to create bold, precise lines.

One of the most common uses for the Brush Tool is in photo retouching. You can use it to paint over areas of the image that need repair, such as removing blemishes or smoothing skin. For detailed digital art, artists often use the Brush Tool to create strokes that mimic traditional painting techniques, such as oil paints or watercolor.

The Clone Stamp Tool is another important tool for editing and repairing images. It allows you to duplicate parts of an image and apply them to another area. This tool is perfect for removing unwanted elements from your photos. For example, if you're working on a landscape and want to remove a distracting object, you can use the Clone Stamp Tool to sample pixels from one area of the image and paint over the object you want to remove. The Clone Stamp Tool is particularly useful for seamless repairs, such as fixing damaged or missing parts of an image. To use it, hold down the Alt key (Option on Mac) to sample an area, then release the key and start painting.

While the Clone Stamp Tool is excellent for duplicating and copying parts of an image, the Healing Brush Tool takes things a step further by blending the sampled area with the surrounding pixels. This tool is perfect for retouching areas like skin or fabric, where you want to maintain texture and shading. The Healing Brush Tool automatically blends the repaired area with the surrounding pixels, ensuring a smooth, natural-looking result. For example, if you're removing acne from a portrait, the Healing Brush Tool can clone healthy skin texture to cover the blemish while matching the surrounding tone and texture seamlessly.

The Content-Aware Fill feature, which works in conjunction with the Healing Brush Tool, allows you to quickly remove objects from an image and have Photoshop fill in the area intelligently. Photoshop analyzes the surrounding content and automatically fills in the removed area to match the background. This is perfect for quickly removing unwanted elements without having to manually clone pixels.

Together, these painting and editing tools offer incredible flexibility and precision for any creative project. Whether you're working on a photo edit, designing graphics, or creating a painting from scratch, these tools provide the power to make seamless adjustments, retouch images, and enhance your work with ease.

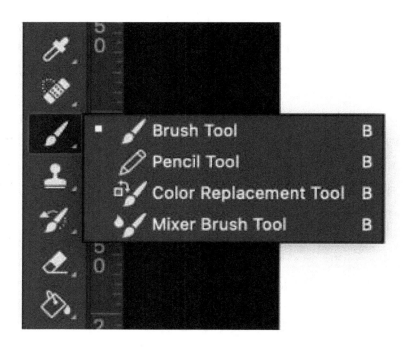

Using the Eraser and Fill Tools

The Eraser Tool and Fill Tool are essential for making quick edits, removing unwanted elements, and filling in areas of your design. The Eraser Tool works similarly to a paintbrush in reverse, allowing you to erase pixels from your image. It can be used to remove parts of a layer or image, and it comes with various options for controlling the size and hardness of the eraser. You can choose from different eraser modes, such as Erase to History, which undoes the most recent change, or Background Eraser, which helps you remove a background while preserving the foreground.

The Fill Tool, on the other hand, is used to fill a selected area with a color or pattern. This tool is often used for quick adjustments, such as changing the color of an object or filling in empty spaces. Photoshop offers different types of fill options, such as Fill with Foreground Color, Fill with Background Color, or even Content-Aware Fill, which intelligently fills the selected area based on the surrounding content.

These tools are incredibly useful for refining your projects, whether you're erasing unwanted areas or filling in empty spaces with solid colors or patterns. By mastering these basic tools, you can quickly enhance your workflow and make your edits more efficient.

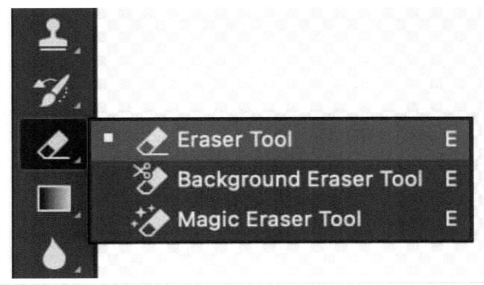

Working with the Gradient Tool

The Gradient Tool is a powerful feature in Photoshop, widely used by designers, photographers, and digital artists to create smooth, seamless transitions between two or more colors. Whether you're designing a subtle background or adding depth to a composition, mastering the Gradient Tool opens up a world of creative possibilities. In this section, we'll explore how to use this tool effectively, walk you through its settings, and provide real-world examples of how gradients can elevate your projects.

At its core, the Gradient Tool is all about color blending. It allows you to create transitions between colors, whether they're soft and subtle or bold and dramatic. To get started, first, select the Gradient Tool from the toolbar. You'll see a gradient bar appear at the top of the screen, which is where you can choose and customize the gradient for your project. Photoshop offers a variety of preset gradients that you can use, but what makes this tool so powerful is the ability to customize your gradients to suit your exact needs.

The gradient bar at the top of your screen is where all the magic happens. By clicking on it, you open the Gradient Editor, where you can modify the colors of the gradient. The Gradient Editor consists of a bar with color stops at either end. These color stops represent the colors at the start and end of your gradient. You can click on these stops to change the colors by selecting from the color palette, or you can even add new color stops to create multi-colored gradients.

To create a smooth color transition, all you need to do is drag the Gradient Tool across your canvas. The direction and length of your drag will affect the gradient's appearance. For instance, a short drag results in a sharp transition, while a longer drag creates a more gradual fade between colors. You can also use the Shift key to constrain the gradient to a straight line, which is useful when you want precise, linear transitions.

Photoshop offers several different types of gradients: Linear, Radial, Angle, Reflected, and Diamond. Each of these modes affects the way the gradient transitions. Linear Gradient is the default, where colors fade in a straight line between two points. The Radial Gradient creates a circular blend from the center outwards, while the Angle Gradient produces a smooth transition in a 360-degree pattern, which can be great for creating effects like lighting. The Reflected Gradient creates a symmetrical blend, often used for mirrored effects, and the Diamond Gradient creates a square-shaped transition, useful for certain types of design elements.

One of the most powerful aspects of the Gradient Tool is the ability to work with multiple gradients at once. You can create complex effects by layering gradients, adjusting their opacity, and changing their blending modes. For example, you might create a soft gradient background with one gradient, and then overlay a radial gradient to simulate a light source. Photoshop allows you to apply multiple gradients to different layers, so you can experiment and adjust them without affecting the rest of your project.

Using gradients with layer masks is another effective technique. By applying a gradient to a layer mask, you can create smooth transitions between different layers of your design. For example, if you have a photo of a sunset and want to add a gradient sky in the background, you can apply the gradient to a mask, allowing the sunset photo to gradually fade into the new background. This technique is often used in photo manipulation and composite work to blend multiple elements seamlessly.

When working with gradients, it's also important to consider opacity. By adjusting the opacity of your gradient, you can create more subtle effects. A gradient with reduced opacity can help create a more natural-looking blend, especially when working with images or textures.

Gradients are not just for backgrounds—they can also be used to create textures, effects, and depth in your designs. For instance, you can use gradients to simulate lighting effects, shadows, or even create the illusion of movement. In digital painting, gradients can be used to add depth to your work, creating a sense of dimension by simulating how light interacts with objects.

Introduction to Layers and Layer Management

When it comes to organizing your projects in Photoshop, layers are your best friend. They're the fundamental building blocks of your work, allowing you to stack different elements on top of each other, making it easier to edit, adjust, and manipulate individual components of your project. Layer management is key to working efficiently in Photoshop, especially as your projects become more complex. In this section, we'll walk you through the basics of using layers, organizing them, and working with layer effects to enhance your designs.

At its most basic, a layer is like a transparent sheet on top of your canvas where you can add content such as images, text, shapes, or paint. Each layer is independent, meaning changes you make to one layer won't affect the others unless you tell Photoshop to do so. Layers allow you to work non-destructively, meaning you can make adjustments and edits without permanently altering the original content.

The Layers Panel, typically located on the right side of the workspace, is where you manage all your layers. In this panel, you can view all the layers in your document, change their order, hide or show them, and adjust their properties. The layer at the top of the stack is the one that appears in front, while the one at the bottom is the one that appears in the background. You can drag and drop layers to reorder them, or use the Ctrl+Shift+] (Windows) or Cmd+Shift+] (Mac) shortcut to bring a layer forward, and Ctrl+Shift+[(Windows) or Cmd+Shift+[(Mac) to send it back.

A key feature of layers is the ability to apply layer effects. Photoshop offers a wide range of effects that can be applied to individual layers, including drop shadows, glows, and bevels. These effects can add depth and dimension to your work, making elements stand out or appear more integrated with the background. For example, adding a subtle shadow to text can give it a sense of realism and make it easier to read against a complex background.

To adjust the opacity of a layer, simply select the layer in the Layers Panel and adjust the Opacity slider at the top of the panel. Lowering the opacity allows you to create transparency effects, which can be useful for creating softer, more subtle elements or blending layers together. Additionally, adjusting the Fill of a layer allows you to control the opacity of only the contents of the layer (such as text or shapes), while leaving the layer effects intact.

Layer Masks are one of the most powerful features in Photoshop. They allow you to hide or reveal parts of a layer without permanently deleting any content. By adding a mask to a layer, you can use a brush or gradient to paint areas of the mask, which will hide or reveal portions of the layer beneath. Layer masks are non-destructive, meaning you can edit them at any time without affecting the original image. This makes them perfect for blending images together, creating smooth transitions, or selectively adjusting different parts of your design.

Another important aspect of layer management is working with groups. As your project grows, it can become difficult to keep track of all your layers. By grouping related layers together, you can organize your workspace and make it easier to navigate your project. To create a group, simply select multiple layers and press Ctrl+G (Windows) or Cmd+G (Mac). You can then collapse the group to save space in the Layers Panel and keep your workflow neat and efficient.

Smart Objects are another essential feature of Photoshop's layer system. A Smart Object is a special kind of layer that contains image data from raster or vector images. You can apply transformations, filters, and adjustments to a Smart Object without permanently altering the original image. This is especially useful when working on complex designs that require multiple edits or transformations. For example, you can apply a filter to a Smart Object, and if you change your mind later, you can easily adjust or remove the filter without losing any image quality.

Managing layers effectively is crucial for working efficiently in Photoshop. Whether you're working on a simple design or a complex multi-layered composition, understanding how to organize and manipulate layers will greatly enhance your workflow and allow you to create more polished, professional projects.

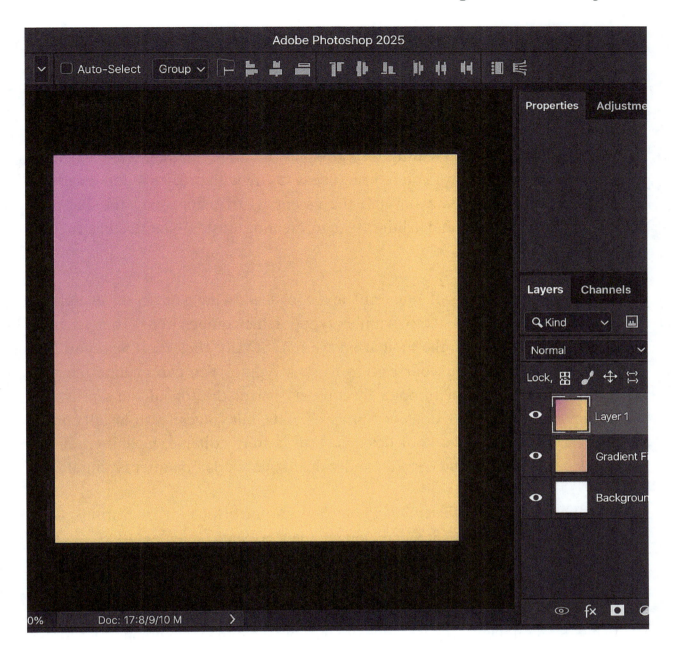

Chapter 3: Working with Text and Shapes

Creating stunning designs is all about combining different elements in ways that are visually compelling and clear. In Photoshop, working with text and shapes is a fundamental skill that opens up endless possibilities for your projects. Whether you're designing a poster, creating web graphics, or simply adding text to a photo, mastering these tools allows you to bring ideas to life with precision and creativity. This chapter will guide you through the essentials of using text and shapes in Photoshop, from adding and editing text to creating custom shapes that fit your vision perfectly.

Photoshop offers a range of powerful text tools, allowing you to do everything from simple type adjustments to complex typographic compositions. To get started, the Text Tool is located in the toolbar on the left. Simply click on it, and you'll be able to click anywhere on your canvas to start typing. You can change the font, size, color, and alignment through the options bar at the top of the workspace. Photoshop comes with an extensive library of fonts, but you can also install custom fonts to further personalize your designs. Text is fully editable, meaning you can adjust the size, spacing, and even the individual letter's position after typing it.

What makes working with text in Photoshop so powerful is its versatility. Once you've typed your text, it's no longer just a static element—it's a fully customizable object. You can apply layer styles like shadows, glows, and bevels to make your text pop. Whether you want your text to stand out with a bold drop shadow or appear smooth and elegant with a subtle glow, the possibilities are vast. By using text effects, you can give your words depth and personality, adding another layer of creativity to your designs.

Along with text, shapes are another crucial part of any design. Photoshop provides a wide variety of shapes that are simple to use and highly effective for creating clean, professional designs. You can use shapes to create backgrounds, buttons, icons, or any other graphic element. The Shape Tool in the toolbar lets you draw basic shapes such as rectangles, circles, and polygons, or you can create more complex custom shapes. Once a shape is drawn, you can customize its color, border, and fill with just a few clicks. The Path Selection Tool allows you to manipulate these shapes and adjust their curves and points, giving you full control over the form and structure of the elements.

What's great about using shapes in Photoshop is the ability to manipulate them in ways that go beyond simple resizing. You can apply gradients, shadows, and even make them interactive, especially when used in web design. By combining different shapes and using tools like Align and Distribute, you can create more intricate designs while maintaining symmetry and balance. Layering shapes on top of each other, and adjusting their opacity, can result in stunning visual effects, perfect for logos, icons, and other graphic elements.

Working with both text and shapes in Photoshop provides an exciting range of creative possibilities. Whether you're adding a title to an image or designing a completely custom logo, these tools let you bring your ideas to life with flexibility and ease. As you become more familiar with these tools, you'll find yourself experimenting with combinations of text, shapes, and other elements to create truly original designs. With the foundation laid, it's time to dive deeper into the creative process and make your projects stand out!

Adding Text to Your Project

Text is an integral part of most design projects, whether you're creating promotional materials, social media posts, or even designing a website. Adding and editing text in Photoshop is straightforward, but it comes with powerful customization options that can elevate your designs to a professional level. Understanding how to manipulate text, select the right fonts, and apply special effects can help you create text that stands out and enhances your overall design.

To begin adding text in Photoshop, first select the Text Tool from the toolbar on the left side of the screen. The icon looks like a capital "T." Once you've selected the Text Tool, click anywhere on your canvas, and a cursor will appear, allowing you to type your desired text. The moment you start typing, Photoshop automatically creates a new text layer in the Layers Panel, which is important because it means you can edit the text independently of the rest of your design.

Once your text is added, the Character Panel will become your best friend. You can adjust the font, size, tracking (the space between characters), and other properties of the text here. Photoshop offers an extensive library of fonts, but you can also import custom fonts to better match your design's style. The Font Selection dropdown at the top of the workspace lets you browse through different fonts, and you can even preview the text in different styles by simply selecting the text in the document.

The font size can be easily adjusted through the options in the Character Panel or by using the Transform Tool (Ctrl+T or Cmd+T on Mac). Increasing or decreasing the font size adjusts how large or small the text appears on the canvas. When adjusting font size, it's important to consider the context of the design—too small, and the text may become hard to read, while too large text can overwhelm the other design elements.

You can also adjust the line spacing (leading), which controls the vertical space between lines of text, and kerning, which is the space between individual letters. These adjustments are key when you want to create more readable or aesthetically pleasing text. For example, increasing the line spacing can help create a more airy, open look, while tightening it can make the text appear more compact and aligned.

Another essential text adjustment is text alignment. Photoshop gives you the flexibility to align your text in different ways—left, right, center, and justify. This can make a huge difference in how your text fits within your design. Center alignment is perfect for titles and headers, while left-aligned text is more natural for body copy. Justified text works well for large blocks of text, like articles or descriptions, giving it a clean, uniform look.

Once you've selected your font, adjusted its size, and aligned it to your liking, it's time to apply special text effects to make it stand out. Photoshop's Layer Styles are a great way to add depth and dimension to your text. These include effects like Drop Shadows, Outer Glow, Bevel & Emboss, and Gradient Overlays. For example, a drop shadow gives the text a sense of depth, making it appear as though it's floating above the background. To apply this, simply click on the fx button at the bottom of the Layers Panel, select Drop Shadow, and adjust the settings, such as the angle, distance, size, and opacity.

Outer Glow is another effect you can apply to text for a vibrant, luminous look. This can be great for titles or headings where you want the text to pop off a dark background. The Bevel & Emboss effect adds a 3D look to the text, which works especially well for logos or text that needs to feel tactile or physical. This effect simulates light and shadow, giving your text the appearance of being raised or recessed.

For text that needs to fit seamlessly into a more stylized design, you can use the Gradient Overlay to apply a smooth gradient across the text, transitioning between two or more colors. This effect can add flair to your text and make it look more dynamic, perfect for creating eye-catching headlines or promotional banners.

Once you have your text looking the way you want, you can fine-tune the overall text positioning. Use the Move Tool (V) to drag your text around the canvas until it fits perfectly with the rest of your design. If you're working with multiple lines of text or different text layers, the Align tools at the top of the workspace are helpful for ensuring everything is neatly aligned to the left, right, or center, or spaced out evenly.

Smart Objects can be used if you plan on transforming the text repeatedly without losing quality. Converting text into a Smart Object preserves its original resolution, allowing you to resize or apply filters without making permanent changes to the text layer. This is ideal for designs that need to be adjusted over time or require multiple versions of the same text in different layouts.

Additionally, Photoshop allows you to apply text effects non-destructively. If you want to add a filter or a more intricate effect, you can convert the text to a smart object first. This gives you the ability to apply filters like Gaussian Blur, Distort, or even artistic effects like Poster Edges without permanently altering your text.

In some cases, you might need to edit the text after you've already added it. Since text is created on a separate layer, you can always return to that text and modify it at any point in your project. Double-click the text layer, and Photoshop will allow you to retype or change the font, size, and effects without affecting the rest of your design.

Once your text is perfected, you can then proceed to integrate it seamlessly with other design elements, whether that involves applying blending modes to give it a more integrated look or using it as part of a larger graphic. By combining these editing techniques, Photoshop allows you to create compelling and professional text designs that stand out and enhance the overall aesthetic of your project.

As you experiment with these features, you'll find that text is not just a functional tool—it's a creative tool in itself, allowing you to communicate messages through style, flair, and design. The more you experiment with different text styles, effects, and layouts, the better your projects will become. The journey to mastering Photoshop text tools will not only make your designs more engaging but will also boost your confidence in creating polished, standout projects.

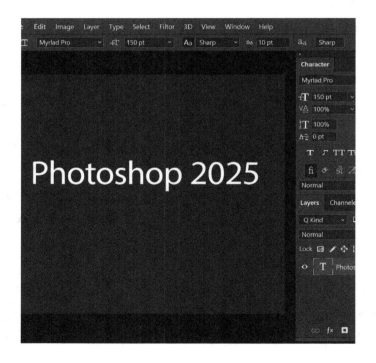

Drawing and Editing Shapes

Shapes are fundamental design elements in Photoshop that allow you to create visually appealing graphics and layouts with ease. The Shape Tool in Photoshop 2025 gives you the flexibility to create geometric figures such as rectangles, circles, polygons, and custom paths. These shapes can be used as standalone design elements or combined to create more complex compositions, making them essential for designers working on everything from logos to web layouts.

To create a shape in Photoshop, first select the Shape Tool from the toolbar on the left side of the screen. By default, the Shape Tool creates a Rectangle, but you can click and hold the Shape Tool icon to reveal a dropdown menu of other shapes, including Ellipse, Polygon, Line, and Custom Shape. The Custom Shape Tool allows you to choose from an extensive library of preset shapes, or you can create your own custom shapes for truly unique designs.

Once you've selected a shape, simply click and drag on the canvas to draw it. Holding down the Shift key while dragging will constrain the proportions of the shape, so you can create perfect squares, circles, or equilateral triangles. For shapes that require more precision, such as polygons, you can enter the number of sides in the top options bar. For example, if you want to create a hexagon, simply set the polygon sides to 6.

One of the most powerful aspects of Photoshop's Shape Tool is the ability to customize the appearance of your shapes. Once you've drawn a shape, it automatically becomes a vector shape, meaning it's made up of paths and anchor points that can be adjusted infinitely without losing quality. You can customize the fill color, stroke color, stroke width, and even the corner radius to give your shape a unique look.

To adjust the fill color, select the shape layer in the Layers Panel and then click on the Fill Color box at the top of the screen. This will bring up a color picker, where you can choose any color from the spectrum or enter a specific hex code for precision. You can also choose gradient fills to give your shape a smooth color transition. Photoshop offers a variety of preset gradients, or you can create custom gradients using the Gradient Editor.

The stroke of a shape refers to its outline. You can adjust the stroke's color, width, and style (solid, dashed, or dotted) to create the desired effect. If you want your shape to have a thicker outline, simply increase the stroke width. If you prefer a more subtle design, you can reduce the stroke width or even remove it entirely. The stroke can also be customized with dashed lines for more dynamic effects, commonly used in logos or designs that require a stylized look.

Another useful feature of the Shape Tool is the ability to round the corners of a shape. If you want to create a softer, more organic appearance, you can adjust the corner radius. This option is especially useful when working with rectangles or squares to create buttons, banners, or other elements that need rounded edges. You can modify the corner radius either by using the sliders or manually inputting a value.

Once you've created and customized a shape, you can use the Path Selection Tool (black arrow) or the Direct Selection Tool (white arrow) to move, resize, and edit the anchor points of the shape. The Path Selection Tool allows you to move the entire shape, while the Direct Selection Tool lets you adjust individual anchor points and curves, giving you precise control over the shape's outline.

Layering shapes is another technique that can add depth and complexity to your designs. By stacking multiple shapes on top of each other, you can create more intricate compositions. The Layers Panel makes it easy to organize your shapes by assigning each one to a separate layer, giving you the flexibility to adjust them independently. You can also apply layer effects like shadows, glows, and bevels to shapes, adding dimension and making them stand out.

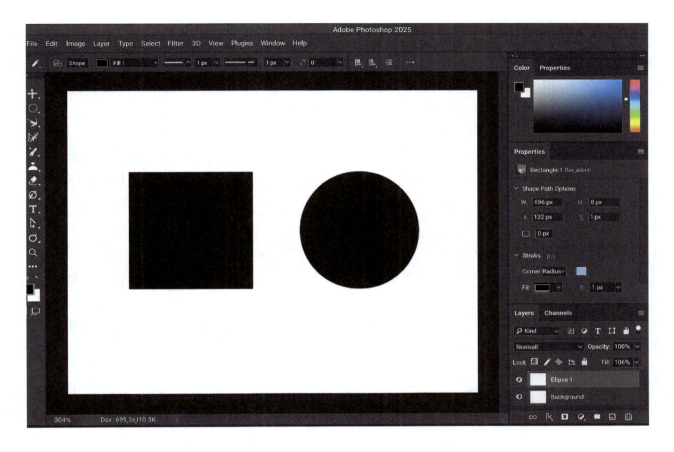

Customizing Text and Shapes Creatively

When it comes to design, the combination of text and shapes opens up a world of creative potential. In Photoshop, you can easily convert text into shapes and apply unique styles, effects, and textures that turn basic design elements into something visually striking. The ability to manipulate text and shapes together allows you to create complex designs, logos, and artistic compositions that feel professional and polished.

One of the first steps in combining text and shapes is learning how to convert text into a shape. This process is useful when you want to manipulate the individual letters as objects and apply effects or transformations that would be difficult to achieve with regular text. To do this, start by creating a text layer using the Text Tool. Once you've entered your text, go to Layer > Type > Convert to Shape. This action converts your text into vector shapes, which can now be resized, rotated, and manipulated like any other shape.

Once the text is converted into a shape, you can break it apart into individual letters or modify the text as a whole. To break apart the text into individual letter shapes, simply select the Path Selection Tool (black arrow) and click on the letter you want to adjust. You can move or resize each letter independently, allowing for custom spacing, alignment, and design variations. If you want to create a dynamic design, you can distort, rotate, or even warp the individual letters to give them more energy and movement.

In addition to editing the individual letters, you can also apply layer styles to your text-shape combination. For example, you could add a gradient overlay to the text to give it a smooth color transition, or apply a stroke to outline the text with a bold color. You can also add drop shadows or glows to make the text pop against the background. These effects can help your text stand out and integrate seamlessly with other design elements.

Combining shapes with text also opens up the possibility of creating unique text effects. For example, you can use shapes as masks to create text that appears to be cut out of an image or texture. To do this, create a shape or image layer, place it above the text layer, and then right-click on the shape layer and choose Create Clipping Mask. This will mask the text with the shape, making it appear as though the text is filled with the content of the shape or image.

You can also combine text and shapes to create interactive design elements such as buttons, icons, and infographics. For example, a circular button can be created with the Ellipse Tool, and then text can be added in the center. You can then apply a gradient fill to the button, and a drop shadow to make it appear 3D. This technique is commonly used in web and app design, where text and shapes come together to form intuitive and visually appealing interfaces.

By combining text and shapes creatively, you can craft sophisticated designs that convey messages in visually compelling ways. Whether you're creating a logo, an advertisement, or just experimenting with design concepts, Photoshop's text and shape tools allow you to explore new ways to express your ideas. The ability to customize and manipulate both elements gives you the freedom to push the boundaries of your creativity and bring your visions to life with precision.

Chapter 4: Mastering Image Adjustments & Enhancements

The ability to make precise adjustments to images is what sets great digital work apart from the rest. Whether you're enhancing a portrait, fixing exposure in a landscape, or tweaking the colors for a more vibrant look, Photoshop's image adjustments and enhancements tools are your secret weapon for bringing your photos to life. This chapter will guide you through the process of fine-tuning your images, ensuring that each element is as vibrant and detailed as it can be. With the right adjustments, your images can go from good to stunning.

Photoshop provides a variety of tools to modify and improve the look of your images, starting with the basics of brightness, contrast, and exposure. These adjustments allow you to control how light or dark an image appears and how much detail is visible in the shadows and highlights. If your image is too dark, increasing the brightness will lighten the entire photo. However, it's important to strike a balance—too much brightness can wash out details. On the other hand, adjusting the contrast changes the difference between light and dark areas, helping the image pop by making shadows deeper and highlights brighter.

For more detailed editing, Photoshop allows you to adjust the levels and curves of an image. The Levels tool provides a way to control the tonal range of your image by adjusting the shadows, midtones, and highlights. This is particularly useful for correcting exposure problems and ensuring that the image looks balanced. If you want more control, the Curves tool gives you even finer adjustments. By manipulating the curve line, you can adjust the image's brightness and contrast at specific tonal points, offering a more tailored way to enhance the image.

When it comes to color adjustments, Photoshop offers powerful tools like the Hue/Saturation and Color Balance tools. The Hue/Saturation adjustment lets you shift the colors in an image, making them warmer or cooler, or completely changing the overall color scheme. The Color Balance tool allows you to adjust the amount of red, green, and blue in the shadows, midtones, and highlights of your image, which is particularly useful for color correction or giving your image a certain mood or tone.

For images that need a bit of a creative touch, Photoshop offers several more advanced adjustment tools. The Vibrance tool is one of these, allowing you to boost the colors of an image without over-saturating skin tones or other delicate areas. Selective color adjustments can also help you fine-tune specific hues in your image, making certain colors stand out without affecting others. Whether you want to enhance the blue sky in a landscape or make the reds in a sunset more vivid, these tools give you the flexibility to make nuanced adjustments.

Another critical feature of Photoshop is the Smart Filters tool. When applied, filters in Photoshop usually make permanent changes to the image, but Smart Filters allow you to apply effects non-destructively. This means you can always go back and adjust the filter's settings or remove it completely. This feature is invaluable when experimenting with effects like Gaussian Blur, Sharpening, or Noise Reduction, as it gives you room to make adjustments without the risk of losing your original work.

Using these image adjustments and enhancements, you can not only correct technical flaws in an image but also infuse it with creativity. Whether you're retouching a photograph, correcting exposure, or enhancing colors, these tools are essential in your Photoshop toolkit. By mastering these adjustments, you can ensure that every image you work on has the perfect balance of light, color, and clarity, resulting in stunning and professional results every time. With these techniques, your creative possibilities are endless, and your images can be transformed into true works of art.

Basic Image Corrections (Brightness, Contrast, Exposure)

When it comes to perfecting an image, one of the first steps is correcting its basic light and color balance. Adjusting Brightness, Contrast, and Exposure are essential tools for enhancing an image's appearance and ensuring it looks just right, whether you're editing a photo for a client or fine-tuning a personal project. These tools can help you correct poorly lit images, improve details, and ensure the tones and colors are balanced in a way that makes the subject pop. This section will take you through the basics of these adjustments and show you how to use them effectively in your workflow.

Brightness Adjustment

Brightness controls the overall lightness or darkness of an image. When an image is too dark, adjusting the brightness can lighten it and make details more visible. Likewise, if an image is too bright and lacks detail in the highlights, reducing the brightness can help restore balance. In Photoshop, the Brightness/Contrast adjustment layer is the simplest way to modify the overall brightness of an image.

To adjust the brightness, go to Image > Adjustments > Brightness/Contrast or use an Adjustment Layer. The Brightness slider lets you lighten or darken the image. Moving the slider to the right increases the brightness, while moving it to the left darkens the image. It's important to adjust this slider carefully, as pushing it too far can result in a washed-out image or a loss of details, especially in the highlights.

For example, if you have a photo of a landscape taken at dusk, the image may appear too dark. Increasing the brightness will reveal the details in the shadowed areas, making the scene more vibrant and clear. However, it's essential to be mindful of not over-brightening, as this can cause the sky or bright areas to lose detail.

Contrast Adjustment

Contrast refers to the difference between the lightest and darkest parts of an image. Increasing the contrast makes the dark areas darker and the light areas lighter, which can give your photo more depth and impact. On the other hand, reducing contrast can result in a more even, flatter image.

In Photoshop, contrast adjustments are typically made using the Brightness/Contrast panel or through Curves or Levels for more precise control. The Contrast slider increases or decreases the intensity of the difference between the light and dark areas. When you increase the contrast, the image may start to look more dramatic, with rich shadows and bright highlights. Reducing contrast, on the other hand, can create a softer, more muted look.

Contrast adjustments are especially useful in portrait photography, where you might want to add depth to the subject's face. For example, if you have a portrait that looks too flat and lacks depth, increasing the contrast will help bring out the features, making the image more striking. However, too much contrast can make the image appear harsh or overly saturated, so moderation is key.

Exposure Adjustment

Exposure refers to the amount of light that hits the camera sensor when the photo is taken, and it directly affects how light or dark the image appears. Correcting exposure is often necessary when an image is either overexposed (too bright) or underexposed (too dark). Exposure adjustments can be especially useful when working with images that were taken in challenging lighting conditions.

In Photoshop, exposure can be adjusted using the Exposure adjustment layer or the Camera Raw Filter. The Exposure slider adjusts the overall exposure of the image, lightening dark areas or darkening bright areas. This tool is particularly useful when you've taken a photo in difficult lighting conditions, such as when the subject is backlit or when shooting in low light.

For example, if you have an image of a cityscape where the bright areas of the sky are overexposed, lowering the exposure can help recover those highlights and bring back the details in the bright portions of the image. Similarly, if an image of a forest is too dark, increasing the exposure will brighten up the shadows and reveal more detail.

Exposure is also closely tied to white balance and color tones. Adjusting exposure can affect how warm or cool an image looks, especially in photos taken in varied lighting conditions. For instance, an overexposed photo may have a cool, washed-out look, while an underexposed photo can appear too warm and murky. Fine-tuning exposure can help achieve a more natural and balanced color tone.

Before-and-After Examples

The real magic of image adjustments comes when you see the transformation that happens when adjusting brightness, contrast, and exposure. Let's say you have a photo of a portrait that looks flat and lacking in detail. By increasing the brightness, the image becomes lighter, revealing details in the shadowed areas. Adjusting the contrast can then add more depth, making the facial features stand out and the background fade into softer tones. Finally, correcting the exposure will bring balance, preventing the bright parts of the image from appearing washed out and ensuring that the photo has a natural, well-lit look.

When making adjustments, it's always helpful to work non-destructively by using Adjustment Layers. These layers allow you to make changes without permanently altering the original image, so you can always go back and tweak the settings if needed.

In the case of an outdoor photo, for example, you might increase the brightness to bring out the details in the dark parts of the landscape. Adjusting the contrast might make the trees and sky stand out more dramatically, while tweaking the exposure can ensure that the sunlight doesn't wash out the scene but still keeps the image vibrant and clear.

It's important to use these tools thoughtfully and adjust the sliders gradually, always checking your image after each change. Sometimes less is more—small adjustments can make a significant difference in how natural or polished the final image appears.

Mastering the basic image corrections of brightness, contrast, and exposure allows you to take control of your photos and ensures that you can enhance and fine-tune each image with precision. These tools are essential for every level of image editing, from basic touch-ups to advanced photo manipulation, and they're the foundation of creating striking, professional-quality visuals.

Using Adjustment Layers (Levels, Curves, Hue/Saturation)

One of the key advantages of working in Photoshop is the ability to make adjustments to an image non-destructively, allowing you to tweak and refine your project without permanently altering the original content. Adjustment Layers are a powerful tool that gives you this flexibility. By using adjustment layers like Levels, Curves, and Hue/Saturation, you can control the light, color, and tone of an image in ways that are easily reversible and can be fine-tuned over time.

Levels Adjustment Layer

The Levels adjustment layer is one of the most commonly used tools for adjusting the brightness and contrast of an image. It works by adjusting the input levels of an image's shadows, midtones, and highlights. Each of these three tonal ranges is controlled through a histogram, which provides a graphical representation of the image's tonal distribution.

To apply a Levels adjustment, go to the Layers Panel and click the New Adjustment Layer icon at the bottom. Select Levels, and a properties panel will appear with a histogram and three sliders: black, gray, and white. The black slider adjusts the shadows, the white slider controls the highlights, and the gray slider modifies the midtones (also called gamma).

By moving the black slider to the right, you can deepen the shadows, making the dark areas of the image darker. Similarly, moving the white slider to the left lightens the highlights, brightening the lighter areas of the image. Adjusting the gray slider modifies the midtones, helping you fine-tune the overall brightness of the image. The Levels tool is excellent for fixing an image that's either too dark or too bright, and by adjusting these three sliders, you can easily improve the contrast and tonal range of any image.

Curves Adjustment Layer

The Curves adjustment layer gives you even more precise control over an image's brightness and contrast than the Levels tool. It allows you to adjust the tonal range in more detail by manipulating a curve that represents the image's tonal values. The curve starts as a straight line, but you can click on it to create control points and adjust the curve to enhance specific areas of the image.

To apply a Curves adjustment, select the Curves adjustment layer from the New Adjustment Layer menu. The Curves panel will appear with a diagonal line running from the bottom left to the top right. By clicking on this line, you can add control points that allow you to adjust the image's tonal range. The bottom left of the curve represents shadows, the middle area represents midtones, and the top right represents highlights.

For example, to brighten an image, you can click on the midtone section of the curve and drag it upward, which lightens the overall image without overexposing the highlights. To deepen shadows, you can click on the shadows area and drag it downward, adding more contrast to the image. Curves allow for more subtle and targeted adjustments, especially when dealing with images that need fine-tuning in specific tonal areas.

Hue/Saturation Adjustment Layer

The Hue/Saturation adjustment layer is a versatile tool for adjusting the color in an image. It controls the hue, saturation, and lightness of an image, allowing you to shift the overall color or enhance specific colors. This adjustment layer is particularly useful for creative effects or correcting color imbalances.

In the Hue/Saturation panel, the Hue slider allows you to shift all the colors in the image. Moving the slider left or right will change the overall color spectrum of the image. For example, moving the Hue slider to the left might shift all the colors toward the blue-green spectrum, while moving it to the right could add more red and orange tones.

The Saturation slider controls the intensity of colors. Increasing saturation will make the colors more vibrant, while decreasing saturation will make the colors more muted, potentially even converting the image to grayscale when fully desaturated. This tool is perfect for enhancing an image's colors or toning them down to create a specific mood.

The Lightness slider adjusts the overall lightness or darkness of the image. This can be useful if you want to lighten the colors in the image without affecting the brightness of the entire photo. You can also target specific colors in the image by clicking the dropdown menu at the top of the Hue/Saturation panel and selecting Reds, Greens, Blues, and other color ranges, allowing you to adjust only specific parts of the color spectrum.

Adjustment layers like Levels, Curves, and Hue/Saturation are invaluable tools for any Photoshop user. They allow for precise and flexible editing of light and color while maintaining the ability to tweak the changes later. By using these adjustment layers, you can achieve professional-quality results while keeping your editing non-destructive and completely reversible.

Retouching and Enhancing Images

Retouching is the process of improving or correcting elements of an image, and Photoshop offers a variety of tools to help you achieve flawless results. Whether you're working on portraits, product photography, or general image enhancements, retouching allows you to fix imperfections, enhance details, and bring out the best in your images. In this section, we'll explore some of the most common retouching techniques, such as removing blemishes, fixing color issues, and enhancing details.

One of the most useful tools for retouching is the Spot Healing Brush Tool. This tool automatically removes blemishes, spots, or other imperfections by sampling pixels around the area and blending them seamlessly. To use the Spot Healing Brush Tool, simply select it from the toolbar, adjust the brush size, and click on the area you want to correct. The tool will automatically blend the surrounding pixels to remove the blemish. For more precise control, you can use the Healing Brush Tool, which allows you to manually sample pixels from a nearby area and apply them to the problem area.

The Clone Stamp Tool is another powerful tool for retouching, especially when you need to remove larger imperfections or duplicate parts of an image. By holding down the Alt key (or Option on Mac) and clicking on the area you want to sample, you can clone pixels and paint them over unwanted areas. This tool is particularly useful for replacing unwanted elements with textures that match the surrounding area.

When it comes to color correction, the Color Balance and Selective Color adjustment layers are your best friends. The Color Balance tool allows you to adjust the overall color tones of the image, shifting it toward warmer or cooler tones. If you're working with a photo that has an unwanted color cast (for example, a greenish tint due to fluorescent lighting), you can use the Color Balance tool to shift the hues and restore a more natural look. Selective Color adjustment gives you more control over specific colors, allowing you to fine-tune reds, yellows, greens, blues, and more.

For sharpening and detail enhancement, Photoshop provides tools like the Unsharp Mask and Smart Sharpen filters. These tools help to bring out fine details and make the image appear crisper. The High Pass Filter is another useful technique for sharpening, where you create a duplicate layer of the image, apply the High Pass filter, and then change the blending mode to Overlay or Soft Light. This method can enhance the overall sharpness of the image without making it look too harsh or unnatural.

Using Dodge and Burn techniques can also help enhance details in an image. Dodge is used to lighten areas, while Burn darkens them. These tools are often used in portrait retouching to enhance the shadows and highlights, adding depth and dimension to the face. You can use the Dodge tool on the highlights of the skin to give it a glowing effect, or use the Burn tool on the shadows to define the cheekbones or jawline.

Retouching doesn't just correct problems—it can also help enhance the beauty of an image, making it more vibrant, detailed, and polished. By mastering Photoshop's retouching tools, you'll be able to fix imperfections, improve lighting, and add creative touches that bring your images to life. Whether you're removing distractions, improving skin tone, or bringing out hidden details, these tools give you the flexibility and control to make your images look their best.

Chapter 5: Working with Layers & Masks

Mastering the use of layers and masks is one of the most essential skills in Photoshop, and it will unlock your ability to create complex compositions with ease. Layers allow you to work on different elements of your project independently, giving you the flexibility to make adjustments without affecting the entire image. When combined with masks, you gain the ability to hide or reveal portions of your work non-destructively, offering a level of control that will take your designs to the next level. Whether you're editing a photo, creating a piece of digital art, or building a composite image, understanding layers and masks is crucial to making your work more dynamic and versatile.

At the heart of any Photoshop project lies the Layers Panel, where all the action happens. Each element in your design, from photos to text to shapes, is placed on a separate layer, allowing you to adjust them independently. Layers provide a way to stack different elements, so you can change one without altering others. For example, if you're working on a composite image with several photos, each photo would be on its own layer, meaning you could move them around, adjust their transparency, or add effects without worrying about affecting the entire project. This flexibility is key to building complex designs that can be easily tweaked.

The true power of layers comes when you start using Layer Masks. A mask is like a magic window that lets you selectively hide or reveal parts of a layer. Imagine you're working on an image with a background that you want to replace. Instead of deleting parts of the image and potentially losing important data, you can use a mask to hide those unwanted sections. The beauty of using masks is that they're non-destructive. If you make a mistake, simply paint back over the mask to reveal the hidden parts again.

Adding a mask to a layer is easy: just select the layer you want to work with, click the Add Layer Mask button at the bottom of the Layers Panel, and you're ready to go. Once the mask is added, you'll be able to paint with black or white on the mask itself. Painting with black will hide parts of the layer, while painting with white will reveal them. You can adjust the brush opacity and flow for smoother transitions or more subtle effects.

Layer masks become particularly useful when you're working on intricate edits or combining multiple images. For example, if you're blending two photos together, using masks allows you to smoothly transition between them without harsh lines. A gradual fade between images can be achieved by using a soft brush on the mask, making the blend seamless. You can also use gradients on the mask to create smooth transitions between layers, such as fading one image into another or gradually adjusting the opacity of an element in the design.

One of the most powerful aspects of working with layers and masks is the ability to combine them with adjustment layers. These layers allow you to modify the properties of the underlying layers, such as brightness, contrast, or color, without permanently changing the image. By adding a mask to an adjustment layer, you can control where and how the adjustments are applied. For example, you might want to brighten only a portion of an image without affecting the rest. Using a layer mask, you can apply that brightness change to just the area you want.

Working with layers and masks also involves knowing how to organize your workflow. When you have many layers, it can get overwhelming. Photoshop allows you to group layers into folders, so you can keep related elements together. For example, you might group all text layers, all image layers, or all shape layers into separate folders. This not only keeps your project organized but also makes it easier to make adjustments when necessary. Additionally, Photoshop lets you adjust the visibility of each layer and adjust the stacking order, which is essential when trying to create complex, layered designs.

By mastering layers and masks, you gain the ability to create designs with precision and flexibility. They are the foundation for almost every project in Photoshop, from simple photo edits to intricate digital artwork. The non-destructive nature of these tools makes them essential for any creative process, allowing you to experiment freely without worrying about making irreversible changes. Layers and masks open up endless possibilities for creativity and are an indispensable part of the Photoshop workflow. As you practice using them, you'll discover just how much control they give you over every aspect of your project.

Introduction to Layers

Layers are one of the most powerful features in Photoshop, allowing you to work on individual elements of your design without permanently affecting other parts of your project. Think of layers as transparent sheets stacked on top of one another— each one containing a different element of your image. Whether you're editing a photo, creating a digital painting, or designing a website layout, layers enable you to make adjustments to specific areas of your project without altering the entire image. This ability to separate elements into layers is what makes Photoshop a versatile tool for all types of design work.

The concept of non-destructive editing is a fundamental advantage of working with layers. Unlike traditional editing methods, where every change is applied directly to the original image (often making it impossible to reverse), Photoshop's layer system allows you to make adjustments, experiment with different elements, and always go back to the original image if necessary. You can hide, delete, or change the order of layers without ever losing the original content. This flexibility is invaluable, especially when working on complex projects with multiple components.

When you open an image in Photoshop, it typically starts as a single background layer. However, as you work, you'll create additional layers, each serving a specific purpose. There are several different types of layers that you will encounter in Photoshop, each offering unique capabilities for different tasks.

- **Text Layers:** These are created when you add text to your image. Text layers allow you to edit the text at any point, adjusting the font, size, color, and style. Text layers are vector-based, meaning they can be resized without losing quality, which is ideal for creating logos, captions, and headlines.

- **Image Layers:** These layers are used to hold images, such as photographs or graphics. When you add an image to Photoshop, it automatically becomes a new layer, allowing you to move, resize, or apply filters and adjustments to it independently of other elements.

- Adjustment Layers: One of the most powerful types of layers in Photoshop, adjustment layers are used to apply changes to an image (like brightness, contrast, or color balance) without permanently altering the original image. Adjustment layers are non-destructive, meaning you can modify or remove the adjustments at any time without affecting the underlying image.

- Smart Object Layers: Smart Objects are layers that contain image data from raster or vector images. They allow you to apply transformations, such as scaling, rotating, and warping, without permanently changing the original image. Smart Objects preserve the quality of your images, making them ideal for repeated transformations or editing.

- Shape Layers: When you draw a shape in Photoshop (e.g., a rectangle or circle), it is placed on a separate shape layer. Shape layers allow you to adjust the properties of the shape, such as color, stroke, and fill, without affecting the rest of the design. You can also easily scale, rotate, and transform shapes without losing quality because they are vector-based.

Each layer in Photoshop can be controlled independently, giving you the flexibility to work on different parts of your project without affecting the rest. For example, you could add a text layer on top of a background image, change the color of the text, and move it around without altering the image beneath it. You can also adjust the opacity of individual layers, allowing you to make them more transparent or more opaque, depending on the desired effect.

Layers also allow you to create complex compositions by stacking multiple elements together. Each layer can have its own set of properties and effects, such as shadows, gradients, or blurs, and these effects can be adjusted separately from the rest of the project. Working with layers is essential when you want to keep your design flexible and easy to edit, especially in more complex projects like photo manipulation, digital painting, or multi-element compositions.

Additionally, layers can be organized into groups. This is especially helpful when working on projects with many layers, as it allows you to keep related elements together for better organization. For example, you could group all of your text layers in one folder, your image layers in another, and any adjustment layers in a separate folder. This makes it easier to navigate your Layers Panel and maintain a clean workspace.

Layer Masks and How to Use Them

Layer masks are one of the most powerful tools in Photoshop, providing a non-destructive way to hide parts of a layer while maintaining its content. Instead of deleting portions of an image or layer, you can use a mask to control the visibility of different parts of that layer. The beauty of layer masks is that they can be edited at any time, allowing you to refine your adjustments or remove the mask altogether without permanently affecting the image.

A layer mask is essentially a grayscale image attached to a layer. The white areas of the mask represent the visible parts of the layer, while the black areas hide the layer. Shades of gray provide varying degrees of transparency, giving you a smooth transition between visible and hidden areas. This allows you to create seamless blends between images, adjust parts of a photo, or apply changes selectively.

To add a layer mask, select the layer you want to apply it to, then click the Add Layer Mask button at the bottom of the Layers Panel. Once the mask is added, Photoshop will automatically display a white thumbnail next to the layer's image thumbnail. The white color means that the entire layer is visible, but as you paint with black on the mask, those areas of the layer will become hidden.

Layer masks can be edited using the Brush Tool, which is the most common method of painting on a mask. To reveal parts of the layer, paint with white; to hide parts of the layer, paint with black. You can also use varying shades of gray for softer transitions between visible and hidden areas. This is especially useful when blending multiple images together, as it allows you to create smooth transitions between them without harsh edges.

For example, if you're creating a composite image and you want to blend the edges of two photos, you can apply a layer mask to the top image and use a soft brush to paint over the areas where the two images meet. By gradually painting with black, you can make the top image fade into the background, creating a seamless blend. The more you practice with layer masks, the more comfortable you'll become with creating smooth and professional-looking transitions between different elements of your design.

One of the most advanced techniques for using layer masks is applying gradients. A gradient applied to a layer mask allows you to create a smooth fade from one layer to another. This can be particularly useful for blending backgrounds, creating vignette effects, or applying selective adjustments to certain areas of an image.

In addition to painting on a layer mask with a brush or gradient, you can also use selection tools to apply masks to specific areas. For example, if you want to apply a mask to just one section of an image, you can use the Lasso Tool or Quick Selection Tool to select the area, then add a mask to hide everything outside of the selected area. This is particularly useful when you need to make selective adjustments or remove unwanted elements without affecting the rest of the image.

Layer masks are an essential part of Photoshop's non-destructive editing workflow. They allow you to make adjustments to your images with precision and flexibility, giving you full control over how elements are revealed or hidden. Whether you're blending multiple photos, adjusting the opacity of a layer, or fine-tuning details in your image, layer masks are indispensable tools for achieving high-quality results in your designs.

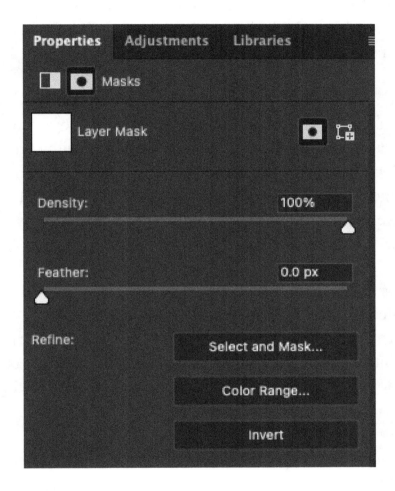

Layer Styles & Effects

One of the key features that elevate Photoshop to a powerful design tool is the ability to apply Layer Styles and Effects. These options provide an easy and flexible way to add depth, dimension, and personality to your designs, whether you're working on typography, icons, or full-blown compositions. Layer styles like drop shadows, bevels, and glows can transform a flat design into something dynamic and visually engaging.

Layer styles are applied directly to the layer, meaning that they can be adjusted, removed, or modified at any time without affecting the original image or layer. This non-destructive process allows you to experiment with different effects and quickly see how they alter the look of your design without committing to permanent changes. Whether you want to add a subtle shadow or create bold, eye-catching text effects, layer styles give you the creative flexibility to enhance your work efficiently.

To apply a layer style, first, select the layer you want to modify in the Layers Panel. Then, click on the fx icon at the bottom of the panel. A list of available effects will appear, including Drop Shadow, Inner Shadow, Outer Glow, Bevel and Emboss, Gradient Overlay, Stroke, and more. Each of these effects adds a unique visual element to your design, and you can customize their settings for different looks.

Let's start with one of the most commonly used effects: Drop Shadow. This effect adds a shadow to the selected layer, making it appear as though it's floating above the background. Drop shadows can help add depth and separate elements from the background, making them stand out more clearly. When applying a drop shadow, you can adjust several settings, including the angle of the light source, the distance of the shadow from the layer, the spread of the shadow, and its size. You can also control the opacity, determining how dark or light the shadow appears.

For instance, if you're designing a button and want to give it a 3D effect, applying a drop shadow can create the illusion of depth, making the button appear as though it's raised above the background. By adjusting the angle of the shadow, you can simulate different light sources, ensuring the shadow falls in the correct direction.

Another popular layer style is Bevel and Emboss, which adds a 3D effect to the selected layer. This effect gives your layer the appearance of being raised or pressed into the surface. It's commonly used for text, icons, and other design elements that need to look like they have depth. The Depth setting controls how prominent the effect is, and the Size setting determines how much the bevel is applied. You can also adjust the Soften setting to smooth the edges of the bevel, giving it a more polished look.

Bevel and Emboss is often used for logos, text effects, or any design element that needs to appear tactile or physical. For example, if you're creating a metallic logo, applying a bevel effect with the right settings can give the text a shiny, reflective quality that mimics the look of polished metal.

Outer Glow and Inner Glow are other commonly used layer styles, particularly for text. An outer glow creates a halo of light around the edges of the layer, while an inner glow gives the appearance of light coming from within the layer itself. These effects can add a touch of brightness to your designs, making them stand out against dark backgrounds or adding a neon-like quality to the text. You can adjust the color, size, and spread of the glow to create the desired effect. A soft glow can add elegance, while a stronger, more defined glow can create a bold, attention-grabbing look.

When applying these styles, don't forget that you can combine them to create even more complex effects. For example, you might apply a drop shadow to your text, add a bevel and emboss for depth, and finish it off with an outer glow for a radiant look. The ability to stack multiple effects in a non-destructive way gives you unlimited creative freedom.

In addition to these core styles, Photoshop also provides more advanced effects, such as Gradient Overlay and Pattern Overlay. These allow you to apply color gradients or patterns to a layer, making them perfect for creating custom backgrounds or adding texture to text and shapes. Stroke is another versatile style that adds an outline around your layer, which can be adjusted in terms of color, size, and position.

The key to mastering layer styles is experimentation. Photoshop's non-destructive nature means you can easily try different combinations of effects to see what works best for your design. Layer styles can be stacked, reordered, and modified at any time, so don't be afraid to experiment with settings until you achieve the desired look. They're essential for designers who want to quickly enhance their work with professional-quality effects while maintaining full control over every detail.

Working with Groups and Adjustment Layers

Managing a project with multiple layers can quickly become overwhelming. That's where layer groups and adjustment layers come in, offering an organized way to handle complex compositions and make non-destructive changes to your image. Photoshop's ability to group layers and apply adjustments to them separately from the original image makes it a powerful tool for creative professionals.

Working with Layer Groups

When you have a lot of layers, especially in a large composition, grouping layers can help keep everything organized. Groups allow you to collect related layers and treat them as a single unit. To create a group, select the layers you want to combine, right-click on one of them, and choose Group Layers or press Ctrl + G (Windows) or Cmd + G (Mac). You'll now see the selected layers grouped in the Layers Panel, and you can collapse or expand the group for easy access.

Layer groups are especially useful when working on designs that involve multiple elements, such as text, images, and shapes. For example, if you're designing a poster with several text elements and images, you can group the text layers together and the image layers together. This organization not only helps keep your workflow clean, but it also makes it easier to move or adjust all elements of the group simultaneously. You can apply transformations, effects, or adjustments to the entire group without affecting individual layers inside it, streamlining your design process.

Additionally, you can add Layer Masks to groups, allowing you to control the visibility of all layers within the group at once. This is useful for blending elements in a more cohesive way, ensuring that the group of layers interacts seamlessly with the rest of your design.

Adjustment Layers

Adjustment layers are a non-destructive way to apply changes to your image's colors, tones, and contrast. Instead of applying adjustments directly to the image layer, which would alter the original pixels, adjustment layers sit above the image layer and allow you to modify the image's properties without permanently changing it. This gives you the flexibility to tweak and refine your design as needed.

To add an adjustment layer, click on the New Adjustment Layer icon at the bottom of the Layers Panel and choose from a list of adjustments, including Levels, Curves, Hue/Saturation, and more. Each adjustment layer affects only the layers below it, and you can adjust the intensity of the effect at any time by double-clicking on the adjustment layer thumbnail.

For example, if you want to adjust the brightness and contrast of a photo, you can add a Brightness/Contrast adjustment layer. This will modify the image's brightness and contrast without affecting the original layer, so you can adjust the settings as needed. If you're working with multiple images, adjustment layers are especially useful for making global changes, such as correcting the overall exposure or color balance of the entire composition.

Adjustment layers can also be masked, allowing you to apply adjustments selectively. If you want to adjust the brightness of just one part of an image, you can apply a mask to the adjustment layer and paint with black to hide the effect in specific areas. This gives you ultimate control over where and how the adjustments are applied, making it an essential technique for photo manipulation and complex compositions.

By mastering layer groups and adjustment layers, you can keep your Photoshop workflow organized, non-destructive, and highly flexible. These tools are essential for designers who want to manage complex projects, maintain control over every aspect of their design, and apply adjustments and effects in a way that can be fine-tuned at any stage of the process.

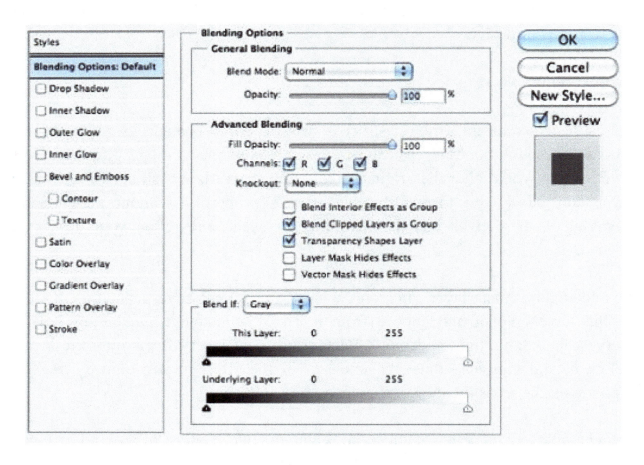

Chapter 6: Advanced Techniques & Effects

The true magic of Photoshop lies in its ability to push the boundaries of creativity. While mastering the basics and understanding the foundational tools is essential, it's when you begin experimenting with advanced techniques and effects that your work truly comes to life. In this chapter, we'll explore some of the more sophisticated features Photoshop has to offer, from advanced blending techniques to creating stunning special effects. These tools are designed to give you the flexibility to transform your images in ways you never thought possible.

As you grow more comfortable with Photoshop, you'll begin to see how powerful layer blending modes and advanced filters can be. These techniques allow you to merge images seamlessly, add texture and dimension, and create effects that would otherwise be difficult or time-consuming to achieve. Photoshop's advanced options like blending modes, layer styles, and filters are key to taking your projects from simple to extraordinary.

One of the most exciting aspects of Photoshop is its ability to manipulate light and shadows. With the Dodge and Burn tools, you can highlight areas of an image, enhancing light spots to bring certain details forward, or darken shadows to create more depth. This technique is commonly used in portrait photography and digital painting to add more dimension to an image. Advanced masking techniques allow you to isolate parts of your design to apply effects selectively, providing full creative control over every element.

Special effects such as glows, bokeh, and liquid or smoke effects take your digital artwork to another level. These effects often require a mix of brushes, layer blending, and smart filters, allowing you to manipulate the environment of your design. Whether you're designing a logo or creating digital art, understanding how to apply and fine-tune these effects will significantly expand your creative toolkit.

Another key element of advanced Photoshop techniques is compositing, the art of combining multiple images into a single, cohesive artwork. Using techniques like seamless blending, perspective corrections, and color matching, you can create complex, realistic compositions that tell a story. Whether you're working on photo manipulation, advertising mockups, or fantasy art, compositing allows you to create eye-catching scenes that seamlessly integrate multiple layers, images, and textures.

As you experiment with these advanced techniques, you'll quickly learn that the possibilities in Photoshop are endless. The software offers a wealth of options that can take your designs to professional-level quality, whether you're working with photos, creating digital illustrations, or experimenting with special effects. The tools may seem complex at first, but with practice, you'll gain the confidence to bring even the most ambitious creative visions to life. As you continue to explore Photoshop's advanced features, you'll discover new ways to express your creativity and develop a unique artistic style that sets your work apart.

Blending Modes

Blending modes are one of the most powerful tools in Photoshop, allowing you to control how layers interact with one another. Essentially, blending modes determine how the pixels of one layer blend with the pixels of the layer beneath it. Each mode offers a different mathematical approach to how pixels are combined, creating a variety of effects that can be subtle or dramatic. By experimenting with blending modes, you can enhance your images, create beautiful effects, and add depth to your designs in ways that are both creative and efficient.

There are many blending modes in Photoshop, and understanding how each one works is key to using them effectively. Let's break down the most commonly used modes and how they can be applied in real-world projects.

The Normal blending mode is the default setting, where the top layer simply covers the layer beneath it without affecting it. This is ideal when you don't need to make any changes to the layer interactions, but you'll find that most of the time, you'll want to explore other modes for more dynamic results.

One of the most versatile modes is Multiply. This mode darkens the underlying image by multiplying the color values of the top layer with the colors of the layer below. It's often used in photo editing to enhance shadows or darken an image while preserving the overall color balance. For example, if you're working with a composite image and want to add a shadow effect to a subject, you can use Multiply to darken only the shadow areas, leaving the rest of the image unaffected.

On the other hand, the Screen blending mode is essentially the opposite of Multiply. It lightens the image by inverting the colors and multiplying them, resulting in a lighter overall appearance. This is especially useful when you want to brighten an image or create highlights. For example, when adding highlights or glowing effects to text or graphics, Screen can be applied to create a soft light effect that brightens the background without overpowering the subject.

For more nuanced blending, Overlay is one of the most frequently used modes. This mode combines the effects of Multiply and Screen, darkening the dark areas of an image while lightening the light areas. It's great for adding texture, enhancing contrast, or creating a more dynamic look. A typical use of Overlay might be to add a textured pattern or design on top of an image without affecting the highlights too much. For example, you could overlay a grainy texture or paper effect on a photo to give it a vintage or textured appearance without losing the detail in the lighter areas.

Soft Light is similar to Overlay, but it provides a more subtle effect. It can be used to gently adjust the brightness or contrast of an image. When you apply Soft Light, it tends to lighten or darken the image depending on the color of the layer. This mode is excellent for enhancing portraits, where you want to add a soft glow or subtle contrast without making harsh changes.

Another very useful mode is Difference, which creates high-contrast effects by subtracting the color values of the top layer from those of the layer below it. It's often used to create dramatic, inverted effects, such as when experimenting with abstract design, photo manipulations, or artistic projects.

To understand how blending modes work in a practical scenario, let's consider a composite image project. Suppose you're combining a cityscape with a portrait and want the portrait to have a softer, more ethereal look. By applying a Soft Light or

Overlay blending mode to the portrait layer, you can merge it with the background, enhancing its vibrancy without overpowering the image. You might also use Multiply on the cityscape layer to darken the image and add a moody feel, especially if you want to emphasize shadows or the night-time ambiance of the scene.

Blending modes aren't just for color adjustments—they can also be used creatively to apply textures and patterns. For example, if you want to add a grunge texture over an image without covering the subject entirely, you can apply a texture layer using the Overlay or Soft Light mode. This will allow the texture to blend seamlessly with the image, giving it a worn, distressed look while maintaining the image's underlying detail.

Ultimately, blending modes are about experimenting and discovering how to create the desired effect. The more you practice, the more natural it will feel to use these modes in your workflow, whether you're enhancing photos, creating digital art, or designing graphics.

Blending Mode	Description	Typical Use	Example Effect
Multiply	Multiplies base color by blend color	Darkening	Enhancing shadows and details
Screen	Multiplies inverse of blend and base colors	Lightening	Brightening images, adding glow
Overlay	Combines Multiply and Screen modes	Contrast adjustment	Adding depth and contrast
Soft Light	Softens the light and dark areas	Subtle lighting effects	Gentle enhancement of image tones

Creating Custom Brushes

Creating custom brushes in Photoshop is one of the best ways to add unique elements to your design work. Photoshop brushes are essentially patterns or shapes that can be applied to a layer in a paint-like manner. Custom brushes allow you to create personalized designs, textures, and effects that can be used repeatedly in your projects. Whether you're adding artistic strokes, creating textures, or drawing complex patterns, custom brushes provide endless creative possibilities.

To create your own custom brush in Photoshop, start by creating a new document or working on an existing one. The first step is to design or select the image you want to use as a brush. This could be anything from a simple shape to a more intricate pattern, like a leaf or a star. Once you've created your design, you need to prepare it for brush use by converting it into a brush preset.

To do this, select the Rectangular Marquee Tool or any selection tool to outline the area of the design that you want to convert into a brush. Once selected, go to Edit > Define Brush Preset, and Photoshop will create a new brush based on the selected area. You can name the brush and save it to your brush library for future use.

Once your custom brush is created, you can access it by selecting the Brush Tool from the toolbar, then clicking the brush preview in the options bar to open the brush panel. In the brush panel, you'll find all the brushes, including the custom ones you've created. Custom brushes can be used just like regular brushes, allowing you to paint with your design or texture on any layer.

To refine and modify your custom brush, click on the Brush Settings panel, where you can adjust various properties such as the spacing, size, angle, and texture. You can also set the flow and opacity to control how much paint is applied with each brush stroke. If you want to create a more dynamic effect, you can set the shape dynamics to adjust the size, angle, or roundness of the brush based on pressure, tilt, or other variables. This makes your brush behave more like a natural paintbrush, responding to your stylus or mouse movements. Custom brushes are incredibly useful for adding texture, pattern, or depth to your designs. For instance, if you're creating a digital painting or illustration, you might design a custom brush that mimics the effect of a paint stroke or ink splatter. You can then use this brush to create consistent textures or effects across your artwork.

Another great application of custom brushes is in creating pattern-based designs. For example, if you're designing a background with repeated shapes or textures, you can create a brush out of a pattern and use it to quickly stamp the design across a layer. This saves time and ensures that the pattern is consistent throughout your project.

Additionally, custom brushes can be used to simulate various real-world textures, such as fur, grass, clouds, or water splashes. By customizing the brush settings, you can create a wide variety of natural effects that bring your designs to life.

The key to mastering custom brushes is experimentation. Start by creating simple brushes, and as you grow more comfortable, experiment with more complex textures and settings. With custom brushes, you can add a personal touch to your projects, making them unique and professional-looking every time.

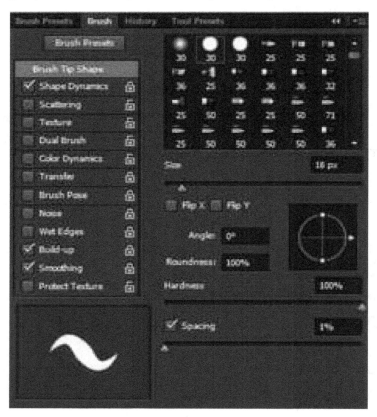

Using Smart Objects

One of the most powerful features in Photoshop for non-destructive editing is the use of Smart Objects. These objects offer a way to work with layers, including images and text, in a way that preserves the original data, giving you the flexibility to make adjustments and transformations without permanently altering the underlying content. Smart Objects are essential for any serious Photoshop user, especially those who want to experiment with different effects, filters, or transformations without losing the integrity of the original layer.

When you open an image in Photoshop or create a new one, it's typically placed on a regular raster layer, which means any transformations (like resizing or rotating) will directly affect the image pixels. However, when you convert a layer into a Smart Object, Photoshop retains the original image data in a way that allows for modifications without damaging or changing the original content. This is incredibly useful for maintaining flexibility in your design workflow.

To create a Smart Object, simply right-click on a layer in the Layers Panel and choose Convert to Smart Object. Alternatively, you can go to Layer > Smart Objects > Convert to Smart Object. Once a layer is converted into a Smart Object, you'll notice a small icon in the bottom-right corner of the layer thumbnail. This icon indicates that the layer is now a Smart Object and can be edited non-destructively.

The primary benefit of Smart Objects is their ability to undergo non-destructive transformations. For instance, if you scale an image on a regular layer, it can lose quality as the pixels are stretched. However, when you scale a Smart Object, Photoshop preserves the original resolution, ensuring that it remains sharp and clear no matter how much you resize it. This is particularly valuable for working with vector-based images, logos, or any artwork that requires frequent scaling, as the resolution remains intact.

In addition to scaling, Smart Objects also allow you to apply filters non-destructively. Typically, when you apply a filter in Photoshop, it permanently alters the layer's pixels. But with Smart Objects, you can apply a filter (such as Gaussian Blur, Sharpening, or Noise Reduction) to the object, and the filter becomes editable. You can double-click the filter in the Layers Panel to adjust the settings, or you can delete the filter entirely if you no longer need it. This flexibility lets you experiment with different effects without committing to permanent changes.

Smart Objects also make it easier to maintain consistency across multiple instances. For example, if you're working with a logo or a graphic that appears multiple times in a design, you can convert the graphic into a Smart Object. If you need to update the design, you can double-click the Smart Object to open it in a new window, make your changes, and save it. The updates will automatically apply to all instances of that Smart Object in your document, saving you the hassle of manually updating each one.

Another key feature of Smart Objects is their ability to handle linked files. You can place a file as a linked Smart Object, meaning that Photoshop will reference the file from an external location instead of embedding it into the document. This can save file size and make it easier to manage multiple versions of the same asset. If the linked file is updated, Photoshop will automatically update the reference in your document, keeping everything in sync without having to manually replace or re-link the file.

Smart Objects also work well when combined with Smart Filters, providing a high degree of control over your image. For instance, you can apply a filter to a Smart Object, adjust the effect, and even use a layer mask to selectively hide or reveal areas of the filter. This allows you to apply complex effects to certain portions of an image, such as blurring the background while keeping the subject in sharp focus. These capabilities make Smart Objects indispensable for advanced editing workflows.

Overall, Smart Objects provide a level of flexibility and precision that makes them essential for high-quality, non-destructive editing in Photoshop. Whether you're working on a composite, creating a design that needs frequent updates, or applying advanced effects, Smart Objects allow you to make adjustments on the fly without worrying about losing original data or image quality.

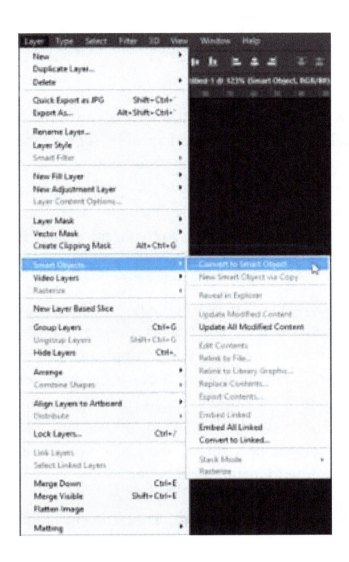

Creating Composites

Creating composites in Photoshop is an advanced technique that allows you to combine multiple images into a single, cohesive piece. Whether you're creating a dramatic scene, blending textures, or combining photos for a marketing campaign, compositing enables you to manipulate and merge various elements to tell a compelling story or enhance a visual. Mastering compositing techniques is essential for anyone looking to create complex, polished digital artwork.

The process of creating a composite begins with selecting the images you want to combine. This could be multiple photographs, digital paintings, textures, or even

3D renderings. The key to successful compositing lies in making these elements work together seamlessly, which requires careful attention to detail in terms of lighting, color matching, and blending.

One of the first steps in creating a composite is cutting out the subjects you want to combine. This can be done using Photoshop's powerful selection tools, such as the Quick Selection Tool, Magic Wand Tool, or Pen Tool. These tools allow you to isolate specific parts of an image and remove the background, so you can place them onto a new backdrop or blend them with other elements. Once you have your subject isolated, it's important to place it on its own layer, so you can adjust it independently of the background.

Next, you'll want to blend the elements together. This is where layer masks come in handy. A layer mask allows you to selectively hide or reveal portions of a layer, giving you the ability to merge two images seamlessly. For example, if you're blending a subject onto a new background, you can use a soft brush on the layer mask to gently blend the edges of the subject, making the transition between the two layers smooth and natural. This technique works best when the subject and background share similar lighting and color tones, but if there's a noticeable difference, you can adjust the colors or lighting to match them better.

Adjustment layers are another powerful tool in compositing. These layers allow you to apply changes to specific areas of the image without affecting the underlying content. For instance, you can use a Hue/Saturation adjustment layer to change the color balance of your subject, making it match the overall tone of the composite. Brightness/Contrast adjustments can help fine-tune the exposure of your layers, and Curves can be used for more precise control over the tonal range of the image.

If the images you're working with don't quite match in terms of lighting, you can use Dodge and Burn techniques to add highlights and shadows, helping to integrate the elements more effectively. By painting with the Dodge Tool (to lighten) and the Burn Tool (to darken), you can add depth to your composite and ensure that all elements appear to be lit from the same light source.

One of the most advanced techniques for compositing is match lighting and perspective. This is especially important when combining elements from different sources, as mismatched lighting can break the illusion of realism. To match the lighting, study the light source in your images and apply gradient maps or adjustment layers to ensure that the highlights and shadows align properly. Perspective matching can also be tricky, but using guidelines or the Vanishing Point Filter can help you align elements to the same perspective grid.

Finally, once your images are seamlessly blended, you can apply final touches to enhance the overall look. Adding texture overlays, sharpening the composite, and applying subtle color grading can tie everything together and make your composite look polished and professional. Using Smart Objects in your composite allows for easy adjustments and flexibility as you make changes to the project.

Creating composites is an essential skill for Photoshop users, especially for those working in fields like advertising, photography, and digital art. By combining multiple images, adjusting them with precision, and using advanced blending techniques, you can create visually stunning and cohesive pieces that have a high level of realism and artistic appeal.

Special Effects

Creating special effects in Photoshop is one of the most exciting aspects of the software, allowing you to add depth, realism, and mood to your projects. Whether you're working on a simple image edit, a complex digital art piece, or a product advertisement, effects like lighting, shadows, and reflections play a huge role in enhancing your design and making it visually striking. These effects can transform a flat, lifeless image into a dynamic and immersive composition, and mastering them will allow you to take your designs to the next level.

Lighting Effects

Lighting is an essential component in every visual medium. It helps set the mood, highlights important elements, and gives the image a sense of depth and realism. Photoshop offers several ways to simulate light and control how it interacts with your images. By using lighting effects, you can create realistic lighting sources that interact with your design elements in a way that mimics real-world illumination.

One powerful tool for adding lighting to your design is the Lighting Effects filter, which can be accessed via Filter > Render > Lighting Effects. This filter offers a variety of light types, including spotlights, point lights, and infinite lights, each affecting the image differently.

- **Spotlight:** This light source mimics a focused beam of light that illuminates a specific part of the image while leaving other areas in shadow. Spotlights are perfect for highlighting a particular subject or detail in your image, such as emphasizing a person in a portrait or a product in an advertisement.

- **Point Light**: Point light is a more omnidirectional light that illuminates the entire image from a specific point. It's often used for simulating natural light sources, such as the sun or a lamp, to create a more evenly lit scene.

- Infinite Light: This type of light is ideal for simulating sunlight, as it comes from an infinite distance. The direction and intensity of the light can be adjusted, making it great for outdoor scenes or when you want to create a broad, even lighting effect.

When applying a lighting effect, you have control over several parameters: light intensity, position, focus, and color. For example, by adjusting the light's intensity, you can simulate different times of the day, such as creating a bright, harsh midday sun or a soft, golden sunset glow. The focus of the light controls how sharp or diffused the light appears, while the position determines the direction from which the light is coming, allowing you to control the placement of highlights and shadows in your image.

Lighting effects can be further enhanced by using gradients, brushes, or layer styles like Outer Glow and Bevel & Emboss. For instance, applying a soft gradient over a background with a soft light layer can simulate a realistic sunlight effect, gradually lightening the top of the image to give the impression of light filtering through the atmosphere.

In portrait work, lighting effects are crucial to shaping a subject's features. By strategically applying highlights and shadows, you can enhance facial features or create a more dramatic look. In digital art, lighting effects can be used to simulate complex light sources, such as glowing objects or light reflections, making the artwork feel more three-dimensional.

Shadows

Shadows are essential for giving objects a sense of depth and making them appear grounded in their environment. Without shadows, objects can feel like they're floating or disconnected from the scene, which can break the realism of your composition. In Photoshop, creating realistic shadows can be achieved in various ways, from simple drop shadows to more complex manual shadows painted on a new layer.

The simplest way to add shadows to your design is through the Drop Shadow effect, found in the Layer Styles panel. Drop shadows are incredibly versatile and can be applied to almost any layer, including text, images, and shapes. By adjusting the distance, spread, and size, you can control how far the shadow extends from the object, how sharp it appears, and how diffused it is. Drop shadows are useful for making text or images stand out against a background, and they're particularly effective when combined with a subtle gradient or a softer shadow.

For more complex shadow effects, such as shadows cast on the ground or around objects, you can create shadows manually. Start by duplicating the object or subject that you want to cast a shadow and placing it on a new layer. Then, use the Transform tool (Ctrl+T or Cmd+T) to distort the duplicated layer, making it look like a shadow falling on the surface below. Once you've positioned the shadow, lower the opacity and apply a Gaussian Blur to soften the edges. This will make the shadow appear more natural, as real-world shadows are rarely sharp and defined.

Another technique for creating realistic shadows is using the Pen Tool to draw out the shadow shapes and then filling them with a dark color. This method works particularly well for creating hard shadows, such as those that appear when a subject is illuminated by a strong, direct light source. Once you've created the shadow, you can adjust its opacity and add a blur effect to soften it.

Shadows can also be used creatively for effect. For instance, long shadows can be used to simulate the effect of low, dramatic light, adding a sense of movement and energy to your design. Alternatively, you can use reflected shadows in a composite scene, such as simulating how objects reflect off a wet surface. Reflections in water, glass, or glossy surfaces can be created by duplicating the object, flipping it vertically, and applying a gradient mask to fade the reflection out.

Reflections

Reflections are another special effect that can enhance the realism of your image and help create depth in your design. Whether you're working on a scene with water, glass, or shiny surfaces, reflections help convey the physical environment and make the scene feel more immersive.

Creating a reflection in Photoshop is simple. First, duplicate the object or image you want to reflect and place it below the original layer. Next, go to Edit > Transform > Flip Vertical to invert the reflection. Position the reflected object appropriately, and then apply a gradient mask to the reflection layer to make it gradually fade out. This simulates how reflections become less distinct the farther they are from the object, which is common in water or glass.

To add a bit more realism, apply a Gaussian Blur to the reflection layer. The degree of blur should match the surface you're simulating—water reflections, for example, tend to have a softer, more diffused look, while reflections in a mirror or window can be sharper.

For added creativity, you can manipulate the reflection with distortion effects to simulate the rippling of water. The Liquify filter or Displace Filter can create realistic water distortions by warping the reflection layer. This technique works well when you want to add more dynamic, organic effects to your composite.

Reflections can also be used in combination with lighting effects. For instance, a reflection on water or glass will often have subtle lighting variations that reflect the surroundings. You can use curves or levels adjustments to tweak the lighting in the reflection, making it consistent with the scene's lighting.

Combining Lighting, Shadows, and Reflections

The true magic happens when you combine all of these special effects—lighting, shadows, and reflections. These effects work together to create a cohesive and visually compelling scene. When you're building a complex image, especially for advertising or digital art, adding each effect step by step ensures that every element of the composition fits together seamlessly.

For instance, imagine you're creating a scene where a product sits on a reflective surface. You would start by placing the product layer, then apply lighting effects to create highlights and shadows on the product. Afterward, you'd add a shadow layer beneath it to ground the object, and apply a reflection effect underneath. By adjusting the opacity, blur, and gradient of the shadow and reflection layers, you can create a harmonious effect that makes the scene feel realistic.

By carefully manipulating each of these elements, you can build a polished, high-quality design that feels rich and dynamic. Lighting can add warmth and focus, shadows can ground elements and create depth, and reflections add an extra layer of realism that makes the entire composition feel three-dimensional.

Whether you're creating a photo manipulation, a product mockup, or digital artwork, mastering these special effects is essential for taking your work from flat to fantastic. With careful application, lighting, shadows, and reflections will not only enhance your designs but also give them a unique sense of dimension and atmosphere that will capture the viewer's attention and leave a lasting impression.

Chapter 7: Retouching and Restoring Photos

Retouching and restoring photos is an art form in itself, and it's an invaluable skill to have in your Photoshop toolbox. Whether you're working on personal photographs, professional portraits, or old family images that need some TLC, the ability to enhance and restore pictures can breathe new life into them. The goal of photo retouching isn't always about changing the image completely—it's about bringing out its best features, fixing imperfections, and preserving memories. This chapter will guide you through the essential techniques and tools in Photoshop that help you perfect your photos, from subtle skin smoothing to major restorations of aged photographs.

We all know that photos often need a little polishing. Whether it's brightening a dull portrait, removing blemishes, or fixing color imbalances, Photoshop gives you all the tools you need to refine your images. Retouching photos allows you to make minor corrections to make your images pop without completely altering the original essence. If you're working on portraits, tools like the Spot Healing Brush and Clone Stamp are perfect for removing minor imperfections like pimples or stray hairs. For more substantial changes, you can use the Dodge and Burn tools to adjust lighting, sculpt shadows, and enhance contrast to make a subject appear more defined.

While retouching focuses on enhancing the present, photo restoration involves bringing old or damaged images back to life. With vintage photos, whether they're faded, torn, or scratched, restoration can turn these fragile memories into clear, vibrant images again. Photoshop's tools such as the Healing Brush and Patch Tool can be incredibly effective at mending old photos. These tools allow you to blend new pixels with the old, ensuring that the repaired areas are as close to the original as possible. The Content-Aware Fill feature is another powerful tool that can automatically replace missing or damaged areas with surrounding textures, allowing for quick fixes without leaving any trace of the original damage.

However, it's not all about erasing flaws—sometimes retouching is about subtly enhancing the beauty of an image. You may want to sharpen details, adjust the lighting, or tweak colors to make a photo feel more vibrant and alive. Adjustment

Layers like Curves, Hue/Saturation, and Levels give you precise control over exposure, contrast, and color balance. These tools allow you to refine every aspect of your image and can be used for both minor tweaks and more significant transformations.

The key to successful retouching and restoration is subtlety. It's about improving the photo without making it look unnatural. Photoshop gives you the flexibility to make non-destructive edits, meaning you can try out different techniques and always revert back to the original image. This flexibility is crucial when restoring old photos, as you can ensure that the final result respects the image's authenticity while also breathing new life into it.

Whether you're improving a modern portrait or breathing new life into a treasured old photo, mastering retouching and restoration techniques in Photoshop is essential for any photo editor or designer. By learning to enhance and repair images with care and precision, you'll be able to create beautiful, timeless photos that capture moments in their best light. With these skills, you'll be ready to transform your photos into something truly exceptional.

Repairing Damaged Photos

When dealing with damaged photos, whether they've suffered from physical wear, such as creases, tears, or discoloration, or digital damage, such as pixelation, it's essential to approach the repair process systematically. Photoshop provides powerful tools like the Spot Healing Brush and the Patch Tool, which can help restore these images to their former glory without compromising their authenticity. The goal of repairing a damaged photo is to preserve its integrity while eliminating imperfections, ensuring the final result is both polished and true to the original image.

The first step in repairing a damaged photo is assessing the extent of the damage. If the photo has visible creases, tears, or large chunks missing, you'll want to begin by fixing those areas. Start by selecting the Spot Healing Brush Tool (J) from the toolbar. This tool is ideal for small imperfections, such as blemishes, scratches, or tiny tears. The Spot Healing Brush works by automatically sampling pixels around the area you're working on, blending them seamlessly to remove the imperfection.

To use the Spot Healing Brush, zoom in on the damaged area, and adjust the brush size to fit the area you want to repair. Simply click on or brush over the imperfection, and Photoshop will fill in the area with nearby pixels. It's helpful to work in small sections to maintain control over the repair process. For larger areas, the Healing Brush Tool (J) can be used, which requires you to sample a nearby area manually by holding Alt (Windows) or Option (Mac) and then painting over the damaged spot.

For larger, more complex repairs, the Patch Tool (J) is invaluable. This tool allows you to select a damaged area and then replace it with pixels from another part of the image that matches in texture and tone. To use the Patch Tool, first, select the damaged area using the Lasso Tool or the Polygonal Lasso Tool. Then, drag the selected area over to a part of the image that is undamaged and has a similar texture. Photoshop will automatically blend the two areas to create a seamless repair.

If the photo has areas where large sections are missing, or if you're working with a torn photo that has visible edges, use the Content-Aware Fill feature. This tool intelligently fills in gaps by analyzing the surrounding pixels and then generating new pixels that blend naturally with the existing image. To use Content-Aware Fill, first make a selection around the area you want to repair. Then, go to Edit > Fill, and choose Content-Aware from the drop-down menu. Photoshop will analyze the selection and automatically fill in the area with the most appropriate pixels.

In cases where the damage has caused significant loss of color or fading, you can use adjustment layers like Hue/Saturation, Curves, and Levels to restore the original color balance. This allows you to fine-tune the tonal range and color balance of the entire image, ensuring that repaired areas blend seamlessly with the rest of the photo.

For areas where the damage is more severe, such as major discoloration or large tears, you may need to combine multiple techniques. Start by using the Patch Tool or Healing Brush for larger repairs, then refine the image using Content-Aware Fill for smaller, hard-to-reach areas. Finish by applying adjustment layers to correct any remaining tonal discrepancies.

As you work through the repair process, always make sure to zoom in closely to ensure you're achieving a smooth, seamless result. Take your time and adjust the settings as needed to achieve the most natural and invisible repairs.

One of the best features of working with Photoshop's repair tools is the non-destructive editing process. All your repairs can be done on new layers or via layer masks, which means you can make changes and adjustments at any time without affecting the original image. This makes the repair process much more flexible and forgiving.

Repairing damaged photos requires patience, precision, and an eye for detail. Photoshop's tools are incredibly powerful, allowing you to restore even the most damaged images with ease. With a little practice, you'll be able to breathe new life into your old photos, whether you're fixing simple wear-and-tear or major damage.

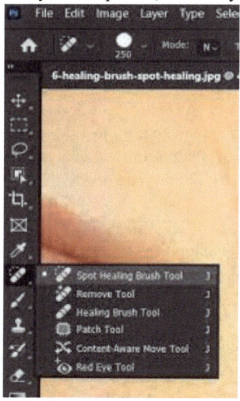

Removing Blemishes and Red-Eye

Removing blemishes and imperfections from photos is one of the most common tasks when retouching portraits. Whether it's skin imperfections, blemishes, or the notorious red-eye that often appears in flash photography, Photoshop gives you a variety of tools to make these corrections while maintaining a natural look. The goal is to enhance the subject's appearance without making the edits obvious, so it's essential to approach this process with care and subtlety.

Let's start with blemish removal. The most commonly used tools for this task are the Spot Healing Brush and the Healing Brush Tool. The Spot Healing Brush is ideal for small imperfections, such as pimples, freckles, or scars. It works by sampling pixels from the surrounding area and blending them into the blemish, making it disappear seamlessly. To use the Spot Healing Brush, simply select it from the toolbar, adjust the brush size to fit the blemish, and click on the area to remove it. Photoshop will automatically blend the surrounding pixels, erasing the imperfection in the process.

If the blemish is larger or more complex, the Healing Brush Tool may be a better option. This tool requires you to manually select a clean area of the skin to sample, which ensures a more precise and natural blend. To use the Healing Brush, hold down Alt (Windows) or Option (Mac) to sample an area, then paint over the blemish. This gives you more control over the source of the pixels, ensuring that the repair blends well with the surrounding skin texture.

For smaller imperfections or subtle skin smoothing, you can also use the Clone Stamp Tool. This tool works similarly to the Healing Brush but allows you to clone specific areas of the image. While it's not as seamless as the Healing Brush, it can be useful when you need to precisely control the area being cloned. To use the Clone Stamp Tool, hold down Alt (Windows) or Option (Mac) to sample a clean area, and then paint over the imperfection.

Another tool for retouching skin is the Patch Tool, which can be used for larger areas that need repairing, such as uneven skin tone or scars. To use the Patch Tool, select the damaged area with the Lasso Tool and then drag it to an area that is free of imperfections. Photoshop will automatically blend the two areas together, creating a seamless repair.

Moving on to red-eye removal, this issue occurs when the camera's flash reflects off the retina, causing the eyes to appear red in photographs. Fortunately, Photoshop has a quick fix for this problem. To remove red-eye, first zoom in on the subject's eyes, then select the Red Eye Tool from the toolbar. Click on the red part of the eye, and Photoshop will automatically correct the color, restoring the natural eye color. If necessary, you can adjust the Pupil Size and Darkness settings to refine the result.

If the Red Eye Tool doesn't fully fix the problem or if you want more control, you can manually adjust the eye color using the Hue/Saturation adjustment layer. Select the Eyedropper Tool to sample the red area, then use the Hue/Saturation adjustment to shift the color toward a more natural tone, such as green or brown.

Lastly, for portraits that need general skin smoothing or evening out of skin tone, the Gaussian Blur and Surface Blur filters can be used to subtly soften skin texture. Apply a Gaussian Blur to the skin areas on a separate layer, then use a layer mask to blend the effect into the surrounding areas. This ensures that the overall look remains natural and doesn't appear overly smoothed or artificial.

The key to successful retouching is subtlety. Aim to enhance the image without making the edits too obvious. With practice, you'll master the art of blemish removal and red-eye correction, and be able to make your photos look natural and polished. These tools will help you restore your photos, making them look fresh and beautiful, while maintaining their original character.

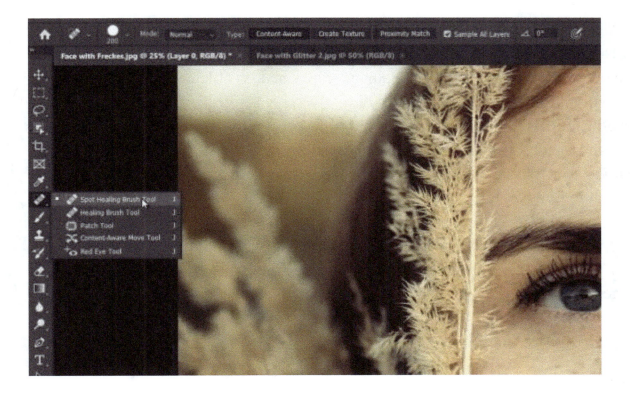

Restoring old photos

Restoring old or faded photos is a delicate process that can breathe new life into cherished memories. Whether you're dealing with a family heirloom that has been passed down through generations or simply trying to salvage an old photo that's been damaged by time, Photoshop provides a powerful suite of tools that can help you restore these images to their original beauty. This chapter will walk you through the process of photo restoration using retouching tools and color correction methods in Photoshop, ensuring that even the most worn-out pictures can be revitalized with care and precision.

Assessing the Damage

Before you begin restoring a photo, it's essential to assess the damage. Old photos may be faded, torn, or discolored. They may also have noticeable stains, cracks, or scratches. The first step is to examine the image carefully, looking at areas that need the most attention. Some of the common issues with old photos include:

- **Fading:** Over time, photos can lose their vibrancy due to exposure to light or environmental factors.

- **Tears and Cracks:** Physical damage can cause visible tears, rips, or cracks, especially in photos that are decades old.

- **Color Shifts:** Photos from older film processes often suffer from color imbalances, such as yellow or magenta casts.

- **Stains or Dust:** Old photos may also accumulate dust, dirt, or stains that are difficult to remove.

Once you've identified the damage, you can begin working on restoring the photo. Let's dive into the tools and methods that will help you repair and enhance your image.

Step 1: Digitize the Photo

Before you can start working on restoring a photo, you'll need to scan or photograph it to bring it into Photoshop. Make sure to scan the photo at a high resolution—300 dpi (dots per inch) is a good standard to ensure that the details of the photo are preserved.

Once you've scanned the photo, open the image in Photoshop. Always work on a duplicate of the original image so that you retain the untouched version in case you need to revert to it later. To create a duplicate, simply press Ctrl+J (Windows) or Cmd+J (Mac), and you'll have an editable copy.

Step 2: Repairing Scratches, Cracks, and Tears

The first major repair task is fixing the physical damage. Scratches, cracks, and tears can be effectively repaired with Photoshop's Spot Healing Brush Tool and Patch Tool. These tools help blend the damaged areas with the surrounding pixels, restoring a seamless and natural appearance.

- **Spot Healing Brush Tool:** This tool is perfect for small scratches or blemishes. Select the Spot Healing Brush Tool from the toolbar, adjust the brush size to fit the damaged area, and simply paint over the scratch or imperfection. Photoshop will automatically sample pixels from the surrounding area to fill in the damaged spot. If the result isn't perfect, you can adjust the area by using the History Brush Tool or by switching to the Healing Brush Tool, which allows for more manual control.

- **Patch Tool:** For larger areas, the Patch Tool is extremely useful. To use it, select the tool, then draw a selection around the damaged area. Once selected, drag the area to a clean part of the image that matches the texture and tone of the original photo. Photoshop will blend the damaged area with the new section, creating a seamless repair. The Content-Aware Fill feature, accessed by selecting an area and choosing Edit > Fill > Content-Aware, can also be helpful for replacing larger areas of damage. Photoshop will analyze the surrounding pixels and fill the damaged area accordingly.

- **Clone Stamp Tool:** If the Patch Tool and Healing Brush tools don't completely blend the damage, you can use the Clone Stamp Tool. Hold down Alt (Windows) or Option (Mac) to select a nearby clean area, and then carefully paint over the damaged sections. This tool is perfect for areas where you need precise control, such as a line in the image or more intricate details.

Step 3: Color Correction

Once you've repaired the damage, it's time to work on the color of the image. Older photos often suffer from fading, which can cause the colors to look washed out or unnatural. In Photoshop, you can use a combination of adjustment layers to restore the photo's vibrancy and correct any color shifts.

- **Levels:** The Levels adjustment is one of the most powerful tools for color correction. It adjusts the tonal range of the image by tweaking the shadows, midtones, and highlights. To use Levels, go to Image > Adjustments > Levels, and adjust the sliders for the shadows, midtones, and highlights until the image looks balanced. If the image has a color cast, you can adjust the individual Red, Green, and Blue channels to correct the overall tone.

- **Curves:** If you need more precise control over the tonal range, the Curves adjustment is a great option. It allows you to control the image's brightness and contrast in specific tonal areas. To use Curves, go to Image > Adjustments > Curves. You can adjust the curve directly on the graph, or you can use the sliders for individual color channels. Curves is particularly useful when you need to adjust an image's contrast while preserving its highlights and shadows.

- **Hue/Saturation**: For color imbalances, such as yellowing or a magenta cast, the Hue/Saturation adjustment layer can be used. This tool allows you to shift the hues of individual colors, making them more natural and balanced. Go to Image > Adjustments > Hue/Saturation, and use the sliders to modify the overall color balance. If certain areas of the image are too saturated, you can also reduce the saturation of individual colors.

- **Selective Color:** If you need to tweak specific colors in the image, the Selective Color adjustment layer is perfect. It allows you to adjust the intensity of individual colors without affecting the entire image. For example, if the image has too much yellow, you can reduce the yellow intensity using the Selective Color panel.

Step 4: Removing Noise and Improving Detail

Old photos often suffer from noise, a type of graininess that can make them look less sharp and less refined. Photoshop has a few powerful tools for reducing noise and sharpening the image.

- **Reduce Noise:** To reduce noise, go to Filter > Noise > Reduce Noise. This will help smooth out the grain and make the image appear cleaner. You can adjust the sliders for Strength, Preserve Details, Reduce Color Noise, and Sharpen Details to find the right balance.

- **Sharpening:** Once the noise is reduced, it's time to bring back some of the sharpness. Use the Sharpen filter or the High Pass Filter to increase clarity and detail. To use the High Pass Filter, duplicate the layer, apply Filter > Other > High Pass, and set the layer blending mode to Overlay or Soft Light. This will enhance the sharpness of the image without creating harsh, unnatural edges.

Step 5: Final Touches

After the major repairs and corrections are done, it's time to add the finishing touches. These may include cropping the image to improve composition, adjusting the contrast to make the image pop, or applying a slight vignette to focus attention on the central subject. You can also add a texture overlay or apply subtle blur effects for artistic enhancement. Use these final steps to polish the image and ensure the restoration looks as natural and cohesive as possible.

Preserving the Restored Image

Once the restoration is complete, it's essential to save the image in a format that retains its quality. If you plan on doing more work with the image in the future, save it as a PSD file to preserve all layers and edits. For sharing or printing, you can export the image as a JPEG or TIFF, depending on the desired quality and file size.

Restoring old photos is a rewarding process that combines technical skill with creativity. By using Photoshop's powerful retouching tools, you can preserve precious memories for years to come, allowing them to be appreciated by future generations. The combination of subtle adjustments and careful restoration can bring new life to damaged or faded photos, restoring not only their appearance but the emotions and stories they carry.

Chapter 8: Working with Photoshop Actions & Automation

Efficiency is the key to mastering Photoshop, and one of the best ways to boost your workflow is by using Photoshop Actions and Automation. These tools allow you to streamline repetitive tasks and apply complex edits with a single click. If you've ever found yourself performing the same series of steps over and over again, actions and automation will become your best friends. Whether you're editing hundreds of photos for a project or applying a consistent effect across multiple images, learning how to harness the power of Photoshop Actions can save you hours of work and give you more time to focus on the creative aspects of your projects.

At the heart of Photoshop Actions is the ability to record a series of steps you perform on an image and then replay them with a single button press. Think of it as creating a custom shortcut for a set of processes. Instead of manually adjusting every layer, applying filters, or making specific edits to each image, you can automate the entire process with actions. Once you've created your action, you can apply it to any open document, ensuring consistency and saving time across projects.

The beauty of Photoshop Actions is their versatility. You can create simple actions for straightforward tasks like resizing or converting images, or more complex actions for tasks such as applying specific effects, retouching photos, or batch processing large groups of files. Photoshop allows you to build a sequence of steps within an action, including image adjustments, layer modifications, filter applications, and even keystroke shortcuts. The more you experiment with Actions, the more you'll discover how customizable they can be to suit your personal workflow or the needs of specific projects.

One of the most useful features of Photoshop Actions is the ability to apply them to batch processing. If you need to resize or format a set of images for a website, apply the same color correction across multiple photographs, or export files in different formats, actions will handle it for you. Photoshop's Batch Processing feature allows you to select a folder of images and apply an action to each one, saving you from performing the same edits manually on every single image.

Photoshop also provides built-in actions that you can use, offering presets for common tasks like sharpening, color correction, and resizing. These default actions can be a great starting point if you're new to the concept of Actions, and you can easily customize them to fit your needs. You can also share your custom actions with others or download actions from various online sources, further expanding the possibilities of automation.

Beyond recording and running actions, Photoshop offers more advanced automation tools, such as Scripts. Scripts allow you to automate more complex tasks that go beyond the basic functionality of actions. For example, scripts can create intricate sequences of edits or integrate Photoshop with other software, such as exporting directly to a website or syncing with an external database. While scripts require a basic understanding of coding, they offer incredible potential for specialized workflows.

The best part about using actions and automation is the time saved, especially when working on large projects. Whether you're a photographer needing to apply batch edits to hundreds of images, a designer applying the same style to multiple pieces, or someone looking to speed up your overall Photoshop process, actions and automation will help you achieve your goals faster and more efficiently. Embrace these tools, and you'll quickly find that Photoshop can work harder for you, leaving you with more time to focus on the creative side of your projects.

Introduction to Actions

Photoshop actions are one of the most efficient tools available to Photoshop users who want to speed up their workflow. If you find yourself performing the same tasks repeatedly in Photoshop, actions can be a game-changer, allowing you to automate steps and apply them to multiple images with a single click. But what exactly are actions, and how can they help you streamline your work?

At its core, a Photoshop action is a recorded sequence of steps that you perform on an image. These steps can range from basic operations, like resizing an image or applying a filter, to more complex workflows, such as retouching, color correction, or even batch processing multiple files. Once an action is created, you can apply it to other images without needing to manually repeat each step. It's like having your own personalized Photoshop shortcut, capable of applying a predefined set of commands automatically.

The beauty of Photoshop actions lies in their flexibility and power. They can be used for simple, repetitive tasks, such as resizing images for web use or creating social media posts, or for more intricate processes, like applying specific effects or adjusting colors. For example, if you frequently apply a specific combination of filters, adjustments, or cropping to images, you can record that sequence and apply it to any number of images with just one click.

In addition to simplifying repetitive tasks, actions also ensure consistency across your projects. If you're working on a series of images that need to adhere to the same visual style, you can record an action that includes all the necessary edits—such as color grading, sharpness, or cropping—and apply it to every image in your series. This helps maintain a consistent look and feel across all your files, which is especially useful for large-scale projects like product photography, marketing materials, or social media campaigns.

But actions aren't just for individuals working on one-off projects. They can also be shared with other Photoshop users. If you've created an action that significantly improves your workflow, you can export it and share it with colleagues or clients, ensuring everyone uses the same process. Likewise, you can download actions from the Photoshop community to enhance your own workflow. The ability to save and share actions makes them even more valuable in collaborative settings.

To start using actions, you need to familiarize yourself with the Actions Panel in Photoshop. This panel is where you can create, organize, and apply actions. In this chapter, we will walk you through the process of recording your own actions, applying them to your images, and even exploring how to set up batch processing for automating tasks across multiple files.

Recording and Applying Actions

Recording an action in Photoshop is simple and straightforward. The first step is to open the Actions Panel, which you can access by going to Window > Actions. This panel allows you to view your existing actions and create new ones. When you're ready to record a new action, click on the New Action button at the bottom of the panel (it looks like a sheet of paper) to create a new set of steps.

Once you've clicked the New Action button, Photoshop will prompt you to name your action and assign it to a set. A set is a collection of related actions, and organizing actions into sets can help you keep your workflow neat and efficient. For example, you might create a set called "Retouching" and another called "Web Processing," grouping actions based on their purpose. You can also assign a function key to your action, allowing you to apply it quickly with a keyboard shortcut.

Now that your action is set up, it's time to start recording. As you perform tasks in Photoshop, every step you take will be recorded in the Actions Panel. For example, if you're resizing an image, Photoshop will record the Image Size change. If you're applying a filter or making color adjustments, those actions will also be recorded. Essentially, Photoshop will log each action you perform, and when you play back the action later, it will repeat those exact steps.

For instance, if you're creating a simple action to resize images for a website, here's how you can do it:

1. Open the Actions Panel and click the New Action button.
2. Name your action, and assign it to a set (such as "Web Processing").
3. Start recording by clicking the Record button in the Actions Panel.
4. Resize the image by going to Image > Image Size and adjusting the dimensions.
5. If desired, apply other adjustments, such as sharpening or color corrections.
6. Once you've completed all the steps, click the Stop button in the Actions Panel to stop recording.

Now, whenever you need to resize an image for the web, you can simply click the Play button on the action, and Photoshop will automatically apply the recorded steps to any image you open. This simple process saves you time and ensures that every image is resized consistently.

But actions can do much more than basic resizing. For instance, you can create actions that apply specific filters, adjust brightness and contrast, apply a vignette effect, or even automate the process of exporting images in multiple formats. The more you experiment with recording actions, the more you'll see how flexible they can be in automating your entire workflow.

Using Batch Processing

Once you've learned how to record and apply individual actions, the next step is to take your efficiency to the next level with batch processing. Batch processing is the ability to apply an action to multiple files at once, saving you even more time, especially when working with large sets of images. For example, if you need to apply a specific filter, resize multiple images, or adjust the color of a set of photos, you can use batch processing to do all of that automatically.

To set up batch processing in Photoshop, you first need to create or select the action you want to apply to your images. Then, follow these steps:

1. Go to File > Automate > Batch. This will open the Batch dialog box.
2. In the Batch dialog box, select the Set and Action you want to apply. If you've already recorded your action, it will be listed here.
3. Under Source, choose where your images are located. You can select a folder or a specific location where the images are stored that you want to process.
4. Under Destination, you can choose whether to save the processed images to a new location or overwrite the existing files. You can also choose to name the files according to your preferences, such as adding a suffix or prefix to the file names.
5. Once you've configured the settings, click OK, and Photoshop will automatically apply the selected action to all images in the source folder.

Batch processing is incredibly useful when working on projects that require consistent edits across multiple images, such as resizing product images for an e-commerce site, applying a watermark, or adjusting the exposure on a set of photos taken under different lighting conditions. By automating these tasks, you can avoid spending hours on repetitive work and ensure that your images are processed consistently.

In addition to resizing or editing images, batch processing can also be used to apply complex adjustments to an entire folder of files, such as converting them to black and white, adding borders, or applying artistic effects. This is particularly valuable when working with large numbers of images, as the time saved by automating the process allows you to focus on the more creative aspects of your work.

For example, imagine you're a photographer working on a project with hundreds of photos. Using batch processing, you could apply a specific color grading action, resize the images to your desired dimensions, and save them in multiple formats, all in one go. This dramatically reduces the time you spend editing and exporting each image individually.

Batch processing can also be combined with Photoshop Scripts for even more advanced automation. Scripts can perform more complex tasks, such as integrating Photoshop with other software or automating processes that actions alone cannot handle. With Photoshop's scripting capabilities, you can create custom workflows that perform intricate tasks across multiple files, making it an essential tool for professionals working in fields like photography, design, and content creation.

By mastering actions and batch processing, you unlock a whole new level of efficiency in Photoshop. Whether you're working on a small set of images or processing hundreds, these tools allow you to automate repetitive tasks and ensure consistency, giving you more time to focus on the creative aspects of your work. The beauty of actions and automation is that they can grow with you—whether you're a beginner or a seasoned pro—helping you streamline your workflow and achieve professional results faster.

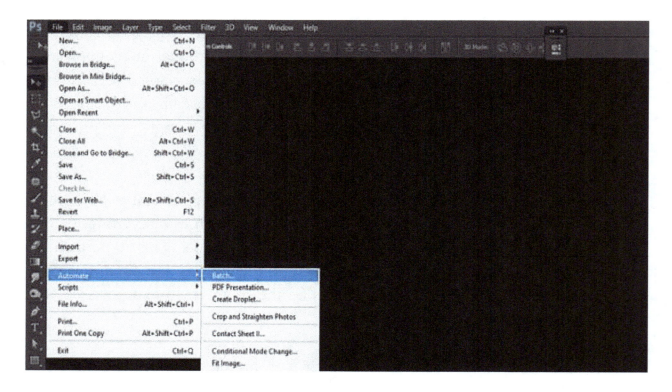

Chapter 9: Creating Graphics for Web and Print

Creating graphics for both web and print is a skill that every designer needs to master, and Photoshop is one of the best tools to help you do just that. Whether you're designing a website banner, a logo, or a flyer, understanding the unique requirements of each medium is crucial to producing professional, high-quality results. The key is to understand how resolution, color modes, and dimensions affect the final product, and how to leverage Photoshop's capabilities to ensure your designs look great no matter where they appear.

For web graphics, the challenge is to create images that are optimized for quick loading times without sacrificing quality. Web graphics are typically displayed on screens, meaning they need to be designed in RGB color mode, which allows for vibrant colors that appear well on digital displays. Photoshop's tools help you adjust your designs for the best possible appearance on screens by enabling you to set the right resolution, typically 72 pixels per inch (PPI), which is ideal for online images. You can also use the Save for Web feature to export your files in a web-friendly format, like JPEG, PNG, or GIF, ensuring that the images are both lightweight and sharp.

On the other hand, print graphics require a different approach. Printing relies on CMYK color mode, which is based on four colors of ink—cyan, magenta, yellow, and key (black)—that are blended together to produce a full spectrum of colors. Understanding the CMYK color model is crucial for ensuring your printed designs look as vibrant and true to the original as possible. Print graphics also need to be designed at a much higher resolution—300 pixels per inch (PPI)—to ensure sharp, crisp images when printed. Photoshop gives you control over these details, ensuring that your designs will look just as good in print as they do on screen.

When creating graphics for both web and print, it's essential to keep in mind the dimensions and proportions of your designs. For web graphics, you'll often need to work with specific sizes based on where the image will be placed—whether it's a social media post, a website header, or a thumbnail. Photoshop allows you to set up artboards or document presets for common web sizes, making it easier to stay consistent across projects. For print, you'll need to consider the print dimensions of the final piece, and make sure your design matches those specifications. In many cases, you may need to set up bleed areas for print, ensuring that the design extends beyond the trim area to account for slight variations in cutting.

The final output is just as important as the design process itself. Photoshop allows you to export your files in the appropriate formats for both web and print. Whether you're optimizing images for fast-loading websites or preparing a detailed brochure for printing, Photoshop's Export As and Save As options help you achieve the best file formats and compression settings for each medium.

Mastering the intricacies of web and print design is a powerful skill that opens up endless creative possibilities. Photoshop's robust set of tools, from resolution adjustments to color mode management, allows you to easily adapt your designs for the specific requirements of any project. With practice, you'll be able to create graphics that not only look stunning on screens but also appear sharp and vibrant in print, helping you create professional and polished designs across all platforms.

Web Graphics: Optimizing for the Web

Designing graphics for the web involves a set of unique considerations that differ from designing for print. Web graphics must be optimized for fast loading, compatibility across various devices and browsers, and clarity in terms of color reproduction. The key aspects to focus on when designing web graphics are resolution, color mode, and file format—all of which impact how the final image is displayed on digital screens.

The first and most critical element when designing for the web is resolution. For web images, a resolution of 72 pixels per inch (PPI) is the standard. This resolution is suitable for screen displays because screens typically display images at a resolution of 72 PPI. Unlike print designs that require much higher resolutions, using 72 PPI for web graphics ensures that the image loads quickly and doesn't unnecessarily consume bandwidth. However, it's important to maintain a balance—high enough resolution to keep images sharp but low enough to maintain fast loading times.

Next, color mode is an essential consideration when designing for the web. The web uses RGB (Red, Green, Blue) color mode, which works based on light. This color model allows for more vibrant, intense colors that display well on screens. The combination of red, green, and blue light in varying intensities creates a wide range of colors. It's crucial to understand the difference between RGB and CMYK (which is used for print) because the colors on a monitor are not always identical to how they will print. When designing web graphics, always ensure that your project is in RGB mode, as this will produce more accurate and vibrant colors on screens.

The file format you choose for web graphics is also a significant factor in optimization. There are a few common formats to consider, depending on the use of the image:

1. JPEG: The most commonly used format for photographs and images with gradients. It allows for smaller file sizes while maintaining a good level of detail, making it ideal for images like photos or complex illustrations.

2. PNG: A lossless format that supports transparent backgrounds. PNG is great for images that require transparency, such as logos, icons, and buttons. While PNGs may have larger file sizes than JPEGs, they maintain image quality without losing detail.

3. GIF: Primarily used for simple graphics or animations. GIFs are limited to 256 colors, making them unsuitable for rich, detailed images but excellent for icons or small web animations.

4. SVG: Scalable Vector Graphics are ideal for simple shapes, icons, and logos. Because SVGs are vector-based, they scale without losing quality and are lightweight, making them perfect for responsive web design.

When designing web graphics, it's important to keep file sizes as small as possible to ensure fast loading times. Large images can slow down websites, negatively affecting the user experience and SEO rankings. To optimize images for faster loading, use Photoshop's Save for Web feature, which lets you adjust compression settings for different formats. JPEG files, for example, can be compressed to a point where the quality remains acceptable, but the file size is much smaller.

Additionally, it's essential to consider responsive design. As web content is viewed across multiple devices, including smartphones, tablets, and desktops, creating graphics that work well across all screen sizes is crucial. For web design, it's important to create scalable assets and export different sizes for different devices (for example, @2x images for high-DPI displays).

Print Design Considerations

Print design differs significantly from web design in several key ways, primarily around resolution, color mode, and file preparation. While web design is optimized for screens, print design needs to consider the physical characteristics of printing, such as paper type, ink limitations, and physical dimensions.

Resolution for print design is much higher than for web design, typically 300 PPI (pixels per inch). This ensures that images remain sharp and detailed when printed. For instance, if you're designing a business card, poster, or brochure, you need to ensure that the images are at 300 PPI, as anything lower would result in a pixelated, blurry print. This high resolution ensures crisp lines and fine detail in print materials.

The color mode used for print is CMYK (Cyan, Magenta, Yellow, Key/Black), which is based on the subtractive color model. Unlike RGB, which uses light to create color, CMYK relies on ink to create colors by subtracting wavelengths of light. When you design for print, it's essential to use CMYK mode in Photoshop because it matches the color mixing process used in printing presses. The colors you see on your screen (which are in RGB mode) will differ from those printed on paper. Photoshop's Proof Colors feature allows you to preview how your RGB design might look in CMYK, helping you to make adjustments for a more accurate print output.

Another important consideration when designing for print is the physical dimensions of the project. Whether it's a flyer, a brochure, or a magazine spread, you need to set up your document in Photoshop to match the size and specifications of the print piece. Photoshop allows you to specify dimensions (in inches or millimeters) and resolution when setting up your file. For print projects, it's critical to work in the exact dimensions that the printer requires to avoid issues with scaling or cropping.

An important factor for print design is bleed. Bleed refers to the extra area around the edge of the design that will be trimmed off during the printing process. Typically, a bleed of 1/8 inch (3mm) is added to ensure that there are no unprinted edges. For example, if you're designing a business card or a magazine cover, you need to extend your design elements slightly beyond the trim line to ensure the print looks seamless after cutting.

Exporting Files for Different Uses

When your design is complete, whether for web or print, you must export your file in the appropriate format and resolution. Photoshop offers a range of options for exporting files, ensuring that your graphics are optimized for their intended use.

For web use, you'll typically export files in formats like JPEG, PNG, GIF, or SVG. Use Save for Web to compress images while maintaining an acceptable quality level, and always check that the file size is appropriate for web use. This is especially important for images used in websites, as large file sizes can slow down load times, which can lead to poor user experiences. To ensure the best result, you may want to create multiple versions of your graphics at different resolutions (e.g., 72 PPI for standard screens, 144 PPI for Retina displays) to ensure they look good on all devices.

For print use, the file should be saved in a high-quality format, such as TIFF or PDF, which preserve image quality. For large print projects, such as banners or posters, you might need to save the file at a higher resolution (300 PPI) and ensure that you've included appropriate bleed settings. PDFs are often preferred for print since they maintain high resolution and support vector graphics, making them ideal for print-ready files.

Additionally, make sure that your CMYK color settings are preserved when exporting for print. This ensures that your colors will print correctly and match your expectations. Photoshop's Export As feature allows you to export files in various formats while ensuring that your design's resolution and color settings are correct.

Finally, keep in mind that both web and print graphics might require specific dimensions. For web graphics, adjust the size according to the platform you're designing for—social media, websites, and email campaigns all have specific size requirements for images. For print, ensure the document dimensions and resolution are set correctly before exporting, so the printer can work with the file without needing further adjustments.

By understanding the unique requirements of both web and print, and mastering Photoshop's export and optimization tools, you can confidently create designs that look great in any medium. Whether you're designing a banner for a website or a flyer for a print campaign, these techniques will help ensure your graphics shine across all platforms.

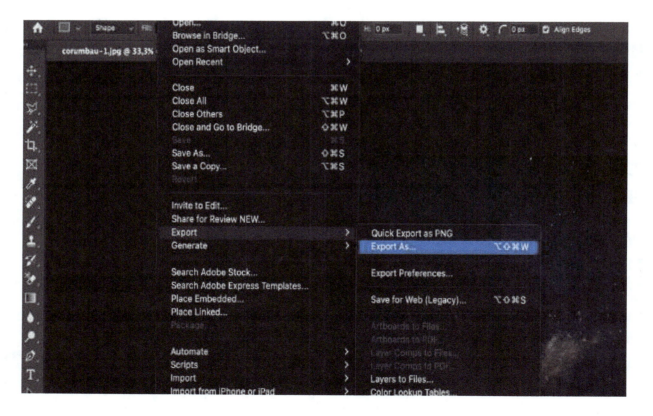

Chapter 10: Troubleshooting and Tips

Sometimes, the most frustrating part of working in Photoshop isn't the design itself but the unexpected issues that arise during the process. From glitches to hidden tools, even experienced designers encounter hiccups that slow down their workflow. Whether you're a beginner or a seasoned pro, knowing how to troubleshoot effectively can save you time and energy, allowing you to continue creating with minimal interruptions. This chapter will guide you through common Photoshop problems and offer tips to help you resolve them quickly, ensuring that nothing stands in the way of your creativity.

One of the most common frustrations in Photoshop is encountering performance issues. These can range from lag when applying filters or transforming layers to the program freezing altogether. One of the first things to check is the performance settings in Photoshop's Preferences. If your system is struggling to keep up, you may need to allocate more RAM or adjust the history states (the number of actions Photoshop remembers). Reducing the number of history states can free up memory and speed up performance, allowing Photoshop to run more smoothly.

Another frequent issue is dealing with unexpected tool behavior. Have you ever tried to use the Brush Tool only to find that it's not working as expected? Sometimes, this can happen if the brush opacity is set too low, or if the brush is on the wrong mode. In cases where the tool simply won't work, it's often helpful to reset the tool to its default settings. Right-click on the tool in the options bar and choose Reset Tool to restore the default behavior. If this doesn't work, check whether your layer is selected properly—sometimes, the tool might be inactive because you're working on a locked or hidden layer.

If your photos aren't displaying correctly or appear pixelated, it could be due to incorrect resolution settings. Make sure that the image resolution is set appropriately for the task at hand—300 PPI for print and 72 PPI for web. If you've started with a low-resolution image, trying to increase the resolution may result in a blurry or pixelated output. Photoshop's Resample option is useful for resizing images, but it's important to understand that upscaling a low-resolution image can only do so much before quality suffers. In these cases, finding a higher-quality version of the image is often the best solution.

Working with layer visibility and blending modes can also lead to frustrating situations. Layers might appear hidden even when they're visible in the layers panel, or they may blend in a way that isn't visually satisfying. One way to troubleshoot this is to ensure that you don't have any accidental layer masks applied, as these can hide parts of a layer. Also, check the blending modes and opacity settings to ensure they are correct. Sometimes, resetting the layer's blending mode to Normal can solve many strange visual issues.

For more complex problems, Photoshop's Preferences panel offers an assortment of tools to reset the program settings. If your brushes, filters, or tools aren't working correctly, it may be time to reset your Photoshop preferences entirely. Hold down Alt + Control + Shift (Windows) or Option + Command + Shift (Mac) as you start Photoshop to reset preferences to their default state. This can solve issues caused by corrupted settings or hidden bugs.

Lastly, it's always important to save your work regularly and back up your files to prevent losing valuable progress. Photoshop can be unpredictable at times, so saving work in increments can prevent hours of rework in case of a crash. Utilizing cloud storage or external drives for backups ensures your designs are safe and secure, even if something goes wrong.

By troubleshooting efficiently and knowing how to fix common issues, you'll be able to keep your creative flow uninterrupted. With a little knowledge and patience, you'll learn to troubleshoot confidently, solving any problem that comes your way while keeping your designs on track. The key is not to get discouraged by the bumps in the road but to see them as opportunities to learn and grow as a designer. Keep experimenting, keep problem-solving, and the next time an issue arises, you'll know exactly how to tackle it.

Common Photoshop Issues and How to Solve Them

Photoshop is an incredibly powerful tool, but like any complex software, it can occasionally throw curveballs your way. Whether you're a seasoned professional or just starting out, encountering issues like crashes, lag, or file corruption is not uncommon. The good news is that most of these problems can be resolved with a bit of troubleshooting and understanding of the software's inner workings. In this section, we'll discuss some of the most frequent Photoshop problems users face and explore effective solutions to get you back to creating.

1. Photoshop Crashes Unexpectedly

One of the most frustrating problems is when Photoshop crashes unexpectedly, causing you to lose your work and wasting valuable time. This can happen for a variety of reasons, including insufficient system resources, corrupted preferences, or incompatible software.

Solution: If Photoshop crashes frequently, start by checking your system's performance. Make sure that your computer meets the minimum system requirements for running Photoshop. Insufficient RAM, hard drive space, or an outdated graphics card can all contribute to instability. Try closing unnecessary applications and background processes to free up resources.

Next, reset Photoshop's preferences. Corrupted preferences can often cause crashes, and resetting them can restore Photoshop to its default settings, potentially solving the issue. To do this, hold Ctrl + Alt + Shift (Windows) or Cmd + Option + Shift (Mac) while launching Photoshop. This will prompt you to reset preferences to their default state. Keep in mind that this will remove any custom settings, so it's a good idea to back up your preferences if needed.

Another useful approach is to disable GPU acceleration. Some crashes occur due to conflicts with your computer's graphics card. To turn off GPU acceleration, go to Edit > Preferences > Performance and uncheck Use Graphics Processor. Restart Photoshop and check if the issue persists.

If none of these steps work, it may be time to reinstall Photoshop. This can resolve any deeper issues caused by corrupted installation files. Before reinstalling, make sure to back up your custom brushes, actions, and presets so you don't lose any important assets.

2. Photoshop Lagging or Slowing Down

If Photoshop is running slowly or lagging, it can seriously hinder your creative workflow. Lag can be caused by a variety of factors, including excessive image resolution, too many open files, or inefficient hardware.

Solution: Start by optimizing your Photoshop preferences for better performance. Go to Edit > Preferences > Performance, and adjust the settings to allocate more RAM to Photoshop. For most users, setting the Memory Usage to 70-80% will help Photoshop run smoother. Reducing the History States and Cache Levels can also improve performance, especially when working with large files.

Another potential cause of lag is having too many open documents or layers. Photoshop can slow down when you have several files open at once, especially if they are high-resolution images. Try to close unnecessary files and reduce the number of layers in each document. Merging layers or using smart objects can also help reduce the strain on your computer's memory.

If you're working with large images or detailed artwork, consider lowering the image resolution while you work. High-resolution images, especially those over 300 PPI, can put a significant strain on Photoshop's performance. You can always revert to the original resolution once your design is complete.

One overlooked cause of lag is the scratch disk. Photoshop uses scratch disks for temporary storage when the available RAM is full. If the scratch disk is full or located on a slow drive, it can cause significant slowdowns. To fix this, go to Edit > Preferences > Scratch Disks and ensure that Photoshop is using a fast, empty drive. If your primary drive is almost full, Photoshop may struggle to access the scratch disk, so make sure you have enough space.

3. Photoshop Files Not Opening or File Corruption

A common issue that can occur when working with Photoshop is the inability to open files or encountering file corruption. Whether it's a PSD file or an image you're trying to edit, this problem can prevent you from accessing important assets, leading to frustration.

Solution: If a file won't open, the first thing to check is whether the file extension is correct. Sometimes files may get saved with the wrong extension or become corrupted during the saving process. Try renaming the file to ensure it has the correct extension (for example, "file.psd" or "file.jpg").

If the file is still not opening, try using Photoshop's "Open as" function. Go to File > Open As and select a different format, such as TIFF or JPEG. This can sometimes bypass any issues with a specific file type. Alternatively, you can try opening the file in another program, such as Adobe Bridge, and then save it in a new format before trying to open it in Photoshop again.

File corruption is a more severe issue, but it's not always the end of the road. If you've encountered a corrupt file, try opening it in Photoshop's Safe Mode by holding Shift while launching the program. Safe Mode disables third-party plugins and custom settings, which might allow the file to open without any external interference.

Another solution is to use Adobe Camera Raw. If your file is a RAW image that is not opening in Photoshop, Camera Raw might be able to process it. Open the file directly in Camera Raw and make adjustments before opening it in Photoshop. Alternatively, Adobe's online repair tool may help recover partially corrupted PSD files.

If none of these methods work, you can also use third-party file recovery software. Some recovery tools are designed specifically for corrupted Photoshop files and may be able to restore your file to a usable state.

4. Photoshop Not Responding or Freezing

Another common issue that users experience is Photoshop freezing or becoming unresponsive, especially when working with large files or complex tasks like filtering or rendering.

Solution: The first thing to do when Photoshop freezes is to give it a moment. Large files or complex actions may take a few minutes to process, so a short pause might resolve the issue. If Photoshop is still unresponsive, try force quitting the program and restarting it. When reopening Photoshop, it might prompt you to recover unsaved work.

If Photoshop continues freezing, check for conflicts with third-party plugins. Some plugins can cause instability in Photoshop. To test this, disable all third-party plugins by going to Edit > Preferences > Plug-ins and unchecking Enable Extensions. Restart Photoshop and see if the issue persists. If Photoshop runs smoothly without the plugins, try disabling each plugin one by one to pinpoint the problematic one.

5. Color Calibration and Display Issues

Sometimes, the colors in your Photoshop design may look different on your screen than they do in print, or the colors may appear distorted when using certain tools. This issue often stems from incorrect color calibration or mismatched color settings between Photoshop and your monitor.

Solution: The first step is to calibrate your monitor. Photoshop's color accuracy depends heavily on your screen's calibration, so using a color calibration tool can help ensure that what you see on screen is what you'll get when printed. You can also adjust your monitor's settings manually using your operating system's display settings.

Next, make sure that Photoshop is using the correct color profile for your project. If you're working on an image for print, ensure you're using the CMYK color mode, and if it's for web, work in RGB mode.

To check and adjust this, go to Edit > Color Settings and make sure that the settings match the specifications for your project.

Photoshop's proofing tools can also help with color discrepancies. Go to View > Proof Setup and select the appropriate profile for your project. This feature allows you to preview how your image will look when printed or displayed on a different device, and it can help you make necessary adjustments before finalizing your work.

Photoshop problems can be incredibly frustrating, but with the right knowledge and troubleshooting techniques, they're often easily solvable. By taking the time to understand the most common issues and their solutions, you can ensure that your work in Photoshop remains smooth, efficient, and enjoyable. Keep these tips in mind, and you'll be able to solve problems quickly, allowing you to focus on what really matters—creating beautiful designs.

How to Recover a Lost File

It happens to the best of us—you're deep into a project, making great progress in Photoshop, and then the unexpected happens: the program crashes or your system shuts down without warning. Suddenly, all that work is seemingly lost. The fear of losing hours of design or editing work can be overwhelming, but don't panic just yet. Photoshop has a few built-in features that can help you recover your unsaved files, and in many cases, it's possible to retrieve your lost work.

The first line of defense against losing unsaved files is Photoshop's AutoSave feature. AutoSave automatically saves copies of your files at regular intervals, ensuring that if your system crashes, you have a recent version of your document to recover. This feature is especially helpful when working on large files or complex projects, where the chances of a crash are higher. To check your AutoSave settings, go to Edit > Preferences > File Handling, and look for the Automatically Save Recovery Information Every X Minutes option. Here, you can adjust the time interval between AutoSave events. If you're working on particularly time-sensitive projects, you might want to set AutoSave to save every five or ten minutes.

If Photoshop crashes unexpectedly and you've lost your work, the first thing to check is whether Photoshop has automatically recovered the file. When you restart Photoshop, it will typically prompt you with an option to recover the file from the last AutoSave. If the recovery option appears, simply select it, and your document will open up with all the recent changes saved. However, AutoSave may not always work if Photoshop is closed manually or if the crash happens before the AutoSave interval has passed. In such cases, don't despair—there are still several options available to you.

If you didn't receive a prompt from Photoshop when restarting, or if you didn't have AutoSave enabled, you can try looking for recovered files manually. Photoshop stores recovery files in a folder on your computer, and depending on your operating system, these files can usually be found in your Adobe Photoshop Recovery folder. The location of this folder varies, but it's typically in your AppData folder on Windows or the Library folder on macOS. Searching for files with the `.psb` extension (Photoshop's recovery files) might lead you to a version of your document that was automatically saved by Photoshop. If you find a recovery file, simply open it in Photoshop, and you may be able to recover the majority of your lost work.

Another option for recovering unsaved files is using the Backup feature in cloud storage services like Adobe Creative Cloud. If you've enabled cloud syncing, you might be able to access previous versions of your file from the cloud. Check the Version History for your file in the Adobe Cloud interface to see if an earlier version is available.

If none of these options work and your file is truly lost, you can also look into third-party file recovery software. These programs scan your computer's hard drive for lost or deleted files, including unsaved Photoshop documents. However, success with these tools isn't guaranteed, and it's important to act quickly before the lost file is overwritten by other data on your hard drive.

In some cases, saving your work regularly and getting into the habit of hitting Ctrl + S (Cmd + S on Mac) frequently can prevent most of these problems. Setting up a regular autosave reminder (even outside Photoshop) can also keep you from losing progress in the future. When working on large or important files, try to save new versions regularly—use a naming convention like "project_v1", "project_v2", and so on, to ensure that even if something goes wrong, you don't lose everything.

Even if all recovery attempts fail, it's important to remember that learning from this experience can improve your workflow moving forward. Always ensure that AutoSave is enabled, back up important files in the cloud, and develop a habit of saving your work frequently to mitigate the risk of future loss.

Tips for Working More Efficiently

Efficiency in Photoshop isn't just about getting your work done faster—it's about working smarter. Whether you're a beginner looking to speed up your workflow or an experienced designer hoping to streamline your process, there are a number of tips and techniques that can help you work more efficiently. By mastering Photoshop shortcuts, utilizing custom workspaces, and optimizing your settings, you can maximize your productivity and focus more on creativity rather than repetitive tasks.

One of the most powerful ways to work more efficiently is by mastering keyboard shortcuts. Photoshop has a vast number of shortcuts that can save you time, whether you're navigating through menus or applying tools. Rather than constantly reaching for your mouse, learn and memorize the most common shortcuts for actions like zooming in and out (Ctrl + + / Ctrl + -), undoing actions (Ctrl + Z), copying and pasting (Ctrl + C / Ctrl + V), and switching between tools (such as Brush Tool (B), Eraser Tool (E), and Move Tool (V)). These shortcuts are simple, but they can save you countless seconds that add up over time.

For those who do repetitive tasks, Custom Shortcuts can take your workflow to the next level. Photoshop allows you to create your own shortcuts for commands that you use frequently. To customize your shortcuts, go to Edit > Keyboard Shortcuts, where you can assign your preferred keys to various actions. For example, if you often need to switch between layers or toggle visibility, you can assign a single shortcut to those commands, allowing you to perform them without taking your hands off the keyboard.

Another key to working efficiently in Photoshop is setting up multiple workspaces. Photoshop allows you to customize your workspace to match the type of project you're working on. Whether you're editing photos, working on illustrations, or designing web graphics, you can set up a workspace that includes only the tools and panels you need for that specific task. To customize your workspace, go to Window > Workspace > New Workspace, and select the panels and tools you want to display. This prevents clutter and makes it easier to focus on the task at hand without constantly searching for tools. You can also save multiple workspaces for different types of projects and switch between them as needed.

Layer Organization is another crucial factor in improving efficiency. As your designs become more complex, keeping your layers organized is essential. Use layer groups to organize related elements and keep your Layers Panel neat. You can also name your layers with descriptive titles to quickly identify them, making it easier to select and modify specific elements. Additionally, don't forget about layer shortcuts. Use the Ctrl + G (Cmd + G on Mac) shortcut to group layers and keep your projects organized.

Another great way to boost efficiency is by mastering Smart Objects. Smart Objects allow you to make non-destructive changes to your design, such as resizing and applying filters, without permanently altering the original image or element. This allows for greater flexibility in your workflow, as you can always go back and adjust the Smart Object later. For instance, if you're working with a logo and you need to adjust its size, doing so with a Smart Object ensures that the quality remains intact, even after multiple transformations.

Actions and Automation are game-changers for repetitive tasks. If you find yourself repeating the same sequence of actions on multiple images, consider recording an action in Photoshop. Photoshop's Actions feature allows you to record a series of steps (such as applying filters, resizing, or renaming files) and play them back with a single click. This is perfect for tasks like batch processing, where you need to apply the same edits to a large number of files. You can also automate your workflow using Batch Processing to apply actions to entire folders of images, saving you considerable time on large projects.

Lastly, consider using layer masks and smart filters to perform non-destructive edits that you can adjust at any time. This not only saves time but also gives you greater control over your designs. For instance, using smart filters allows you to tweak effects like blurring, sharpening, or color adjustments long after they've been applied, offering flexibility and saving you from having to redo your work.

By incorporating these tips and tools into your workflow, you can significantly speed up your design process while maintaining a high level of creativity and accuracy. Photoshop's power lies not only in its features but also in how efficiently you use those features. With a few simple adjustments to your habits and setup, you'll be able to work faster, smarter, and more creatively, making your time in Photoshop even more productive and enjoyable.

Chapter 11: Final Thoughts and Next Steps

The journey you've taken through Photoshop's many tools, techniques, and tricks has only just begun. Mastering Photoshop is not an overnight feat—it's a continual process of learning, experimenting, and refining your skills. You've already built a solid foundation, and now it's time to take the next step toward becoming an even more proficient and confident designer.

The world of Photoshop is vast and ever-evolving, with new updates, plugins, and features regularly being added. While this can seem overwhelming at times, it's also an exciting opportunity for growth. The skills you've gained throughout this guide will serve as your toolkit, but the real magic happens when you apply what you've learned to real-world projects. Whether you're designing graphics for a website, editing photos, or creating digital artwork, you'll now have the confidence to take on any challenge that comes your way.

It's important to remember that Photoshop is not just about knowing how to use the tools—it's about creativity and problem-solving. As you continue working, don't hesitate to experiment with new techniques, explore different workflows, and push the boundaries of what you can create. The beauty of Photoshop lies in its versatility, and the more you practice, the more comfortable you'll become with the software's powerful capabilities.

One of the next steps on your journey is to find your niche within Photoshop. Whether you prefer photo manipulation, digital painting, web design, or any other specialty, honing your skills in a specific area will help you become an expert and stand out in a crowded field. The key to success is practice and persistence. As with any craft, the more you work with Photoshop, the more natural it will feel, and the better your results will be.

Another exciting next step is to join the Photoshop community. The world of design is constantly changing, and being part of a community can keep you informed about the latest trends, tips, and tutorials. Online forums, social media groups, and websites dedicated to Photoshop are great places to share your work, get feedback, and learn from others. Collaboration is an essential part of growth, and engaging with other creatives can open up new ideas, inspire you, and push you to reach new heights.

Lastly, always keep learning. Photoshop has an immense amount of depth, and even the most seasoned professionals are always discovering new ways to use the software. Take advantage of tutorials, workshops, and online resources to expand your knowledge and sharpen your skills. Whether it's exploring new features, mastering shortcuts, or experimenting with new design techniques, there is always room for improvement. Your next big breakthrough could be just around the corner.

As you look ahead, remember that you are equipped with the tools to succeed. Photoshop is your canvas, and with time, dedication, and a spirit of exploration, the possibilities are endless. Keep experimenting, keep creating, and most importantly, keep having fun with your designs. The future of your Photoshop journey is bright, and your creativity has no limits.

Final Tips for Mastery

Mastery of Photoshop doesn't happen overnight, but with consistent effort and focused practice, you can continue refining your skills and achieving remarkable results. This journey is about more than simply knowing how to use the tools—it's about understanding the creative possibilities they unlock and learning how to apply them effectively in various design scenarios.

Throughout this guide, you've explored the essential tools and techniques that form the foundation of Photoshop proficiency. From creating and manipulating images to mastering advanced techniques like working with layers, masks, and smart objects, you've gained a solid understanding of Photoshop's vast capabilities. The key to mastering the software, however, lies not in memorizing tools, but in developing a deep understanding of how to approach different projects with confidence and creativity.

One of the most important things to remember is that practice is the key to mastery. Photoshop is a tool that thrives on experimentation. Every time you open Photoshop and begin a new project, you have an opportunity to try something new, refine a technique, or improve your workflow. Practice doesn't just mean repeating the same steps, but also challenging yourself with new concepts and projects. The more you expose yourself to new challenges, the more you grow as a designer.

Another important aspect of mastery is the ability to simplify your approach. As you gain confidence in Photoshop, you might be tempted to use every tool available to create complex designs. However, some of the best designs come from a minimalist approach where fewer tools are used with more precision. Learning when to stop adding layers, effects, or adjustments can be just as valuable as knowing how to use Photoshop's more advanced features. The ability to step back and evaluate your design with a critical eye is a skill that develops with experience.

In addition to honing your technical skills, developing your design sensibility is also crucial. Photoshop is a powerful tool, but it's your creativity and understanding of design principles—such as color theory, typography, and layout—that will elevate your work. Design is about solving problems and communicating messages effectively, so focus on building your knowledge of design theory alongside your technical expertise. Experiment with different styles, seek inspiration from other designers, and pay attention to how visual elements interact. This balance between technical skill and creative insight is what sets exceptional designers apart.

If you feel like you've reached a plateau or that progress is slow, it's helpful to take a break and step back. Sometimes, a fresh perspective is all you need to see a solution you've missed. Don't be afraid to put a project down for a day or two and come back with new ideas. Creativity can't be rushed, and stepping away from your work can lead to breakthrough moments. Along with patience, learning to embrace constructive feedback is also a valuable practice. Whether it's from peers, mentors, or online communities, feedback can help identify areas for improvement and refine your approach to design.

Lastly, don't forget that design is an evolving field, and Photoshop is constantly evolving with it. There's always something new to learn, from the latest features in each Photoshop update to fresh trends in design aesthetics. Whether you're working on illustrations, photo editing, or web design, there is always an opportunity to grow and push your creative limits. If you keep an open mind and remain curious, you'll find that your journey with Photoshop is filled with constant learning and growth.

Keeping Your Skills Up-to-Date

As a Photoshop user, your journey doesn't stop once you've learned the basics or even mastered the intermediate techniques. The world of design is constantly evolving, and Photoshop, as a leading tool in the creative industry, is updated regularly with new features and improvements. In this fast-paced landscape, keeping your skills up-to-date is crucial for staying competitive and continuing to produce cutting-edge work.

The first step in keeping your skills fresh is to stay informed about new updates and features in Photoshop. Adobe frequently rolls out new versions of Photoshop with exciting tools, improved workflows, and added functionalities. To ensure you're making the most out of your software, take the time to explore new features with every update. Adobe often releases feature highlight videos and tutorials on their website and YouTube channel, so you can get up to speed with what's new. Keeping an eye on these updates can help you discover tools you might not have known about that could improve your workflow and expand your creative possibilities.

In addition to software updates, the design world itself is constantly changing. New trends emerge, design practices evolve, and fresh techniques become popular. Staying current with design trends not only enhances your creative work but also ensures that your designs remain relevant. Follow design blogs, social media accounts, and websites that highlight the latest trends and techniques. Websites like Behance, Dribbble, and Adobe Live are excellent places to find inspiration, learn new techniques, and see how others are using Photoshop in innovative ways.

Participating in these communities can also offer feedback and foster connections with other professionals, which is a valuable resource for growth.

Another powerful way to stay up-to-date is to participate in online courses and tutorials. Many platforms like LinkedIn Learning, Udemy, and Skillshare offer courses specifically tailored to advanced Photoshop users. These resources dive deeper into niche topics, such as photo manipulation, typography, digital painting, and even video editing in Photoshop. Whether you prefer self-paced courses or live workshops, there are a wealth of options available to help you sharpen specific areas of your skill set.

You can also subscribe to design magazines, newsletters, and online publications that feature articles, interviews, and case studies with leading professionals in the industry. Resources like CreativeBloq, Designmodo, and A List Apart offer ongoing education on design trends, Photoshop techniques, and other creative tools. By dedicating time each week to staying informed through these platforms, you'll be able to maintain a cutting-edge understanding of both Photoshop and the broader design landscape.

To truly master Photoshop and keep your skills current, you should also join design communities and engage with other users. Being a part of forums or groups like those found on Reddit, Facebook, or Photoshop-specific communities like the Adobe Photoshop Facebook Group allows you to ask questions, share your work, and learn from others. Getting involved with these communities can expose you to new methods, tools, and tricks that you might not come across otherwise. Plus, interacting with fellow designers allows you to build a network of peers who can provide invaluable feedback and guidance as you continue learning.

Experimenting with different workflows and embracing cross-disciplinary learning are also great ways to keep your skills sharp. Consider learning about areas of design outside of Photoshop, such as web design, motion graphics, or user experience design (UX). Photoshop can be a versatile tool when used alongside other software such as Adobe Illustrator, InDesign, or After Effects. Expanding your skillset to include other design tools and techniques can open new doors to creative possibilities, allowing you to take on more complex projects and broaden your client base.

Finally, one of the best ways to ensure continuous improvement is by challenging yourself with personal projects. Set creative goals for yourself, whether it's a weekly challenge to redesign a logo, create a photo manipulation, or even participate in design competitions. These self-imposed projects not only help you apply what you've learned but also keep you engaged with new techniques and ideas. Plus, they can serve as a portfolio piece to showcase your skills to potential clients or employers.

Keeping your Photoshop skills up-to-date is an ongoing process, but by staying proactive in your learning, engaging with the creative community, and seeking out new resources, you can continue to grow as a designer. With Photoshop's vast array of tools and possibilities, there's always something new to discover, and the more you push yourself to learn, the more exciting the journey becomes. Keep experimenting, stay curious, and always be open to new ideas—your growth as a designer is only limited by your willingness to continue evolving.

Conclusion

As you reach the end of this guide, it's important to reflect on the journey you've taken through the world of Adobe Photoshop. From mastering the basic tools to diving into advanced techniques, you've gained a wealth of knowledge that will empower your creative work for years to come. The tools, tips, and methods explored throughout this book are just the beginning—Photoshop is a tool that evolves with you as a designer, and the possibilities are limitless.

It's easy to become overwhelmed by the sheer power and versatility of Photoshop, but remember: mastery comes with time, practice, and experimentation. The more you engage with the software, the more natural your workflow will become. Each new project you tackle is an opportunity to refine your skills and discover new ways to use Photoshop. Don't be afraid to make mistakes—each one is a valuable lesson that contributes to your growth as a designer.

As you continue your Photoshop journey, remember to embrace your creativity and allow yourself the freedom to experiment with new techniques. Photoshop is not just about following tutorials or knowing the right shortcuts; it's about expressing yourself and finding innovative solutions to design challenges. Keep exploring, keep learning, and keep pushing the boundaries of what you can achieve.

The design world is constantly evolving, and so are the tools that shape it. By staying curious and adaptable, you'll continue to stay ahead of the curve and maintain your creative edge. Whether you're working on personal projects, client work, or exploring new artistic ventures, Photoshop will be there to help you turn your ideas into reality.

Finally, always remember that the journey doesn't end here. Continue to challenge yourself, seek out new resources, and connect with other designers. Photoshop is more than just a tool—it's a gateway to endless creative possibilities. Your next masterpiece is waiting for you to unlock it.

Keep experimenting, keep creating, and most importantly, keep enjoying the process. The world of Photoshop is yours to explore. Happy designing!

Appendices

Appendix A: Photoshop Shortcuts

One of the most effective ways to increase your efficiency in Photoshop is by mastering keyboard shortcuts. These shortcuts not only speed up your workflow but also reduce the amount of time spent navigating through menus. Photoshop, being a powerful and versatile software, offers a wide range of shortcuts across different categories such as tool shortcuts, editing shortcuts, and navigation shortcuts. By using these shortcuts, you'll be able to work faster and more effectively, making your design process smoother and more enjoyable.

Tool Shortcuts

- V – Move Tool: This is one of the most essential tools in Photoshop, allowing you to move layers, selections, and guides around the canvas.
- M – Marquee Tool: The Marquee tool is used for making rectangular or elliptical selections.
- L – Lasso Tool: The Lasso tool allows for freeform selections, letting you draw around the areas you want to select.
- W – Magic Wand Tool: Use the Magic Wand tool to select areas of similar color.
- C – Crop Tool: The Crop tool is used to trim, straighten, and resize your images.
- I – Eyedropper Tool: This tool is used for sampling colors from your image.
- B – Brush Tool: Use the Brush tool for painting on your image.
- E – Eraser Tool: The Eraser tool is used to erase parts of your image or layer.
- G – Gradient Tool: The Gradient tool is used to apply color gradients to your image.
- H – Hand Tool: The Hand tool is used for panning or moving the canvas around while working.
- R – Rotate View Tool: This allows you to rotate the canvas, helping you work with precision in various orientations.
- T – Type Tool: The Type tool is used for adding text to your design.
- U – Shape Tools: The U key selects the shape tool for creating vector shapes like rectangles, circles, and lines.

- P – Pen Tool: This tool is essential for creating precise paths and shapes in your designs.

Editing Shortcuts

- Ctrl + Z (Cmd + Z on Mac) – Undo: The Undo shortcut allows you to reverse your most recent action.
- Ctrl + Shift + Z (Cmd + Shift + Z on Mac) – Redo: Redoing an action you previously undid is as simple as this shortcut.
- Ctrl + C (Cmd + C on Mac) – Copy: Use this shortcut to copy selected elements or layers.
- Ctrl + V (Cmd + V on Mac) – Paste: After copying, use this to paste the copied content.
- Ctrl + X (Cmd + X on Mac) – Cut: This shortcut allows you to cut out content from your project.
- Ctrl + D (Cmd + D on Mac) – Deselect: Deselect any current selections in your project.
- Ctrl + T (Cmd + T on Mac) – Transform: This shortcut opens up the transformation options for resizing, rotating, or adjusting an object or layer.
- Ctrl + J (Cmd + J on Mac) – Duplicate: Use this shortcut to quickly duplicate a layer or selected area.
- Ctrl + E (Cmd + E on Mac) – Merge Layers: Merge the selected layers into a single layer.
- Ctrl + Shift + I (Cmd + Shift + I on Mac) – Invert Selection: This shortcut inverts the current selection, allowing you to quickly work with different areas of an image.
- Ctrl + U (Cmd + U on Mac) – Hue/Saturation: Open the Hue/Saturation adjustment dialog to modify the colors of your image.
- Ctrl + B (Cmd + B on Mac) – Color Balance: Adjust the color balance of your image using this shortcut.
- Ctrl + M (Cmd + M on Mac) – Curves: The Curves tool allows you to adjust the brightness and contrast of your image using a graph.
- Ctrl + L (Cmd + L on Mac) – Levels: Use this to adjust the shadows, midtones, and highlights of your image.

Navigation Shortcuts

- Spacebar – Hand Tool (temporary): Hold down the spacebar while working to quickly switch to the Hand tool for panning.
- Ctrl + + (Cmd + + on Mac) – Zoom In: Use this to zoom into the image, allowing for finer details to be edited.
- Ctrl + - (Cmd + - on Mac) – Zoom Out: Use this shortcut to zoom out and get a broader view of your workspace.
- Ctrl + 0 (Cmd + 0 on Mac) – Fit to Screen: This shortcut quickly adjusts the zoom level to fit the entire image within the Photoshop window.
- Ctrl + 1 (Cmd + 1 on Mac) – Actual Pixels: This shortcut zooms the image to 100%, showing it at actual resolution.
- Ctrl + R (Cmd + R on Mac) – Rulers: Toggle the rulers on and off to help guide your design process.

Layer Shortcuts

- Ctrl + Shift + N (Cmd + Shift + N on Mac) – New Layer: Quickly create a new layer with this shortcut.
- Ctrl + G (Cmd + G on Mac) – Group Layers: This shortcut groups selected layers into one folder, making it easier to manage multiple layers.
- Ctrl + Shift + G (Cmd + Shift + G on Mac) – Ungroup Layers: Ungroup layers that were previously grouped together.
- Alt + Ctrl + G (Option + Cmd + G on Mac) – Create Clipping Mask: This shortcut creates a clipping mask, which restricts the visibility of a layer to the shape of the layer beneath it.
- Ctrl + Shift + E (Cmd + Shift + E on Mac) – Merge All Visible Layers: This merges all visible layers into one layer, making your file more manageable.

Mastering these shortcuts can make your Photoshop workflow more efficient, saving time and minimizing the need to switch between tools or menus. The more familiar you become with these shortcuts, the smoother your experience in Photoshop will be, ultimately allowing you to focus more on creativity rather than manual tasks.

Appendix B: Glossary of Terms

Whether you're new to Photoshop or a seasoned user, the language of design can sometimes feel like a different world. From layers and masks to blending modes and vector graphics, understanding Photoshop's terminology is key to becoming a more confident user. This glossary will help you familiarize yourself with common Photoshop terms and jargon, ensuring that you can navigate through tutorials, resources, and your own projects with ease.

- **Adjustment Layer:** A non-destructive layer used to apply color or tonal adjustments to your image. These layers affect all layers beneath them but do not permanently alter the original image.
- **Artboard:** A canvas or workspace used to design multiple layouts or pages in one document, often used in web and mobile design projects.
- **Bitmap:** A type of image made up of pixels, commonly used in digital photography and other raster-based graphics.
- **Blending Mode:** A setting that determines how a layer interacts with the layers beneath it. Common blending modes include Multiply, Overlay, and Screen.
- **Clipping Mask**: A technique used to constrain the visibility of a layer to the shape or content of the layer beneath it. This allows you to apply effects to a specific area.
- **Crop:** The action of removing parts of an image by adjusting its boundaries. Cropping helps focus on the main subject and improve composition.
- **Destructive Editing:** Any editing or modification to an image that permanently alters the original data, such as flattening layers or applying direct edits to pixel data.
- **DPI (Dots Per Inch):** A measure of image resolution, often used in print design. Higher DPI (typically 300) results in sharper prints.
- **Layer Mask:** A non-destructive way to hide or reveal portions of a layer by painting with black or white. Layer masks are key for blending and compositing.
- **Raster:** An image made up of pixels, usually used for photographs or detailed artwork. Raster images lose quality when scaled up.
- **Resolution:** The amount of detail an image holds, measured in PPI (pixels per inch) or DPI (dots per inch). Higher resolution means more detail.

- **Smart Object:** A layer that contains image data from raster or vector images. Editing a Smart Object is non-destructive, allowing for resizing or applying filters without altering the original image.
- **Vector:** A type of image that uses mathematical paths rather than pixels, allowing for infinite scaling without loss of quality. Common in logos and illustrations.

This glossary covers just a fraction of Photoshop's extensive terminology, but these terms will give you a solid foundation to start building your design vocabulary. As you continue working with Photoshop, you'll undoubtedly encounter even more terms and techniques that will help you expand your skills.

Appendix C: Troubleshooting Checklist

Photoshop is a robust software that allows for incredible creativity, but like any program, it can run into occasional issues. Whether it's a crash, a tool that isn't working as expected, or a file that won't open, knowing how to troubleshoot can save you time and frustration. Use this checklist to identify common problems and resolve them quickly so you can get back to creating.

1. Photoshop Won't Start:
   - Check if your computer meets the system requirements for Photoshop.
   - Try restarting Photoshop in Safe Mode (hold Shift while launching).
   - Reset Photoshop's preferences by holding Ctrl + Alt + Shift (Windows) or Cmd + Option + Shift (Mac) while opening the program.

2. Photoshop Freezes or Becomes Unresponsive:
   - Try to force quit and restart Photoshop.
   - Close unnecessary files or programs running in the background.
   - Check your performance settings (Edit > Preferences > Performance) and allocate more RAM or adjust history states.

3. Tools Not Responding:
   - Reset the tool by right-clicking on the tool icon in the toolbar and selecting Reset Tool.

- Make sure the correct layer is selected, and it's not locked or hidden.
- Check the tool's settings in the options bar (e.g., opacity, size).

4. File Won't Open:

- Verify the file format and extension.
- Try opening the file using File > Open As and select a different file format.
- If the file is corrupted, try Photoshop's recovery options or use file recovery software.

5. Crashes or Errors:

- Check for any Photoshop updates and install the latest version.
- Disable third-party plugins or reset the plugins to see if they're causing issues.
- Check the scratch disk settings and ensure there is enough space on the drive.

6. Color Issues (RGB vs. CMYK):

- Ensure the correct color mode is selected for your project (RGB for web, CMYK for print).
- Use Proof Colors (View > Proof Setup) to simulate how colors will appear when printed or displayed on different screens.

By following this checklist and addressing these common issues systematically, you can keep your workflow smooth and avoid disruptions that might otherwise slow you down. Troubleshooting can sometimes seem daunting, but once you become familiar with the typical problems and their solutions, you'll be able to resolve issues quickly and continue creating without stress.